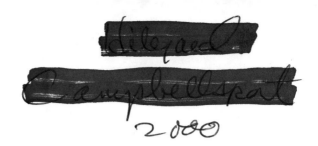

Ruth

INTERPRETATION
A Bible Commentary for Teaching and Preaching

INTERPRETATION

A BIBLE COMMENTARY FOR TEACHING AND PREACHING

James Luther Mays, *Editor*
Patrick D. Miller, *Old Testament Editor*
Paul J. Achtemeier, *New Testament Editor*

KATHARINE DOOB SAKENFELD

Ruth

 *A Bible Commentary*
for Teaching and Preaching

John Knox Press
LOUISVILLE

Scripture quotations from the New Revised Standard Version of the Bible are copyright © 1989 by the Division of Christian Education of the National Council of the Churches of Christ in the U.S.A. and are used by permission. Italic emphasis has been added in some quotations.

Library of Congress Cataloging-in-Publication Data

Sakenfeld, Katharine Doob, 1940–
    Ruth / Katharine Doob Sakenfeld.
        p.   cm. — (Interpretation, a Bible commentary for teaching
    and preaching)
    Includes bibliographical references.
    ISBN 0-8042-3149-4 (alk. paper)
    1. Bible. O.T. Ruth—Commentaries.   I. Title.   II. Series.
BS1315.3.S25   1999
222' .35077—dc21   99-38152

© copyright Katharine Doob Sakenfeld 1999
This book is printed on acid-free paper that meets the American
National Standards Institute Z39.48 standard. ♾
99 00 01 02 03 04 05 06 07 08 — 10 9 8 7 6 5 4 3 2 1
Printed in the United States of America
John Knox Press
Louisville, Kentucky

SERIES PREFACE

This series of commentaries offers an interpretation of the books of the Bible. It is designed to meet the need of students, teachers, ministers, and priests for a contemporary expository commentary. These volumes will not replace the historical critical commentary or homiletical aids to preaching. The purpose of this series is rather to provide a third kind of resource, a commentary which presents the integrated result of historical and theological work with the biblical text.

An interpretation in the full sense of the term involves a text, an interpreter, and someone for whom the interpretation is made. Here, the text is what stands written in the Bible in its full identity as literature from the time of "the prophets and apostles," the literature which is read to inform, inspire, and guide the life of faith. The interpreters are scholars who seek to create an interpretation which is both faithful to the text and useful to the church. The series is written for those who teach, preach, and study the Bible in the community of faith.

The comment generally takes the form of expository essays. It is planned and written in the light of the needs and questions which arise in the use of the Bible as Holy Scripture. The insights and results of contemporary scholarly research are used for the sake of the exposition. The commentators write as exegetes and theologians. The task which they undertake is both to deal with what the texts say and to discern their meaning for faith and life. The exposition is the unified work of one interpreter.

The text on which the comment is based is the Revised Standard Version of the Bible and, since its appearance, the New Revised Standard Version. The general availability of these translations makes the printing of a text in the commentary unnecessary. The commentators have also had other current versions in view as they worked and refer to their readings where it is helpful. The text is divided into sections appropriate to the particular book; comment deals with passages as a whole, rather than proceeding word by word, or verse by verse.

Writers have planned their volumes in light of the requirements set by the exposition of the book assigned to them. Biblical books differ in character, content, and arrangement. They also differ in the way they have been and are used in the liturgy, thought, and devotion of the church. The distinctiveness and use of particular books have been taken into account in decisions about the approach, emphasis, and use of space in the commentaries. The goal has been to allow writers to develop the format which provides for the best presentation of their interpretation.

The result, writers and editors hope, is a commentary which both explains and applies, an interpretation which deals with both the meaning and the significance of biblical texts. Each commentary reflects, of course, the writer's own approach and perception of the church and world. It could and should not be otherwise. Every interpretation of any kind is individual in that sense; it is one reading of the text. But all who work at the interpretation of Scripture in the church need the help and stimulation of a colleague's reading and understanding of the text. If these volumes serve and encourage interpretation in that way, their preparation and publication will realize their purpose.

The Editors

AUTHOR'S PREFACE

The book of Ruth has led me, followed me, at times haunted me over much of my scholarly life. It was first a place to practice proper identification of feminine verb forms in my beginning study of Hebrew language. Its key vocabulary played a prominent role in my dissertation research. Later it became a testing ground for expanding my methodological academic tool kit, as I added rhetorical and literary inquiry to the historical-critical and form-critical approaches I had learned in graduate school. Eventually this story took on new dimensions of promise and difficulty as a key text in Euro-American discussions of feminist biblical hermeneutics. Most recently, it has served as my entry point for cross-cultural sharing of feminist Christian reflection in various Asian settings.

Through these last two aspects of my work, especially in my experiences in Asia, the theological power of this story in the community of faith has become apparent in new and often unexpected ways. Sometimes that power works for ill in women's lives, and this realization led me on a journey something like Naomi's, from a homeland of simple satisfaction with the story, to a distant land in which the story seemed to bring only death and emptiness, and eventually back again to a renewed but changed appreciation of its underlying witness to women's initiative and its vision of human wholeness. The commentary seeks to guide readers through these different ways of experiencing the story by giving explicit attention to alternative interpretations. More thematic exploration of these feminist and cross-cultural concerns can be found in my several recent essays cited in the Bibliography.

The most visible dialogue partners in the commentary itself are of course those scholars whose works are cited. In fact, however, a host of other partners is invisibly but powerfully present, partners who may never have published anything about Ruth (or anything at all) but who have offered profound insights into the book. Among those who deserve special thanks for their contributions through discussion of the material are pastors at gatherings in Minneapolis, Dubuque, Honolulu, and St. Louis; colleagues during my stay at the Center of Theological Inquiry; and most especially the lay and theologically trained women of the Philippines, Korea, Japan, Taiwan, Hong Kong, Thailand, and Myanmar who gave unstintingly of their time as we laughed and wept and laughed again in our struggle with this story.

I am grateful to the trustees of Princeton Theological Seminary for sabbatical time and for a research grant in support of my travel to Asia.

Generous funding also came from the Association of Theological Schools and the National Council of the Churches of Christ in the U.S.A.

Series editors James Mays and especially my colleague Patrick Miller have been patient and encouraging beyond what an author has a right to expect. Marietjie Odendaal gave essential assistance in checking and rechecking citations through several recensions of the manuscript. My "Early Bird" women's prayer and Bible study group has been steadfast in its belief in the worth of the effort to complete the project, as has my mother, Hilda Smith Doob. My thanks go also to dear friend Eugenia Bishop, at whose Vermont cottage most of the writing was accomplished.

This volume is dedicated with honor and affection to the late Helma Edda Ažiņš Sakenfelds, my mother-in-law, and to my husband Helmārs Pēteris Sauldots Sakenfelds; it is from them that I have learned most about what is at stake in emigrating from one's native place to live as a foreigner in a new land.

Remembering
Helma Edda Ažiņš Sakenfelds

Honoring
Helmārs Pēteris Sauldots Sakenfelds

CONTENTS

Introduction

"And they all lived happily ever after." The story of Ruth has been a favorite of many Christians and Jews throughout the centuries. In the midst of scriptures filled with war and the threat of war, with trickery and treachery among brothers and among sisters, with attempts at genocide and brutal reprisals, with disobedience and unfaithfulness, the book of Ruth has been viewed as an island of tranquility in which people generally act well toward one another and the community celebrates a happy ending for all concerned. It is the perspective of this commentary that such a reading is in the end theologically appropriate. Care and concern for others, at times going even beyond the bounds of usual human responsibility, leads in the providence of God to greater wholeness in this microcosm of the human community.

At the same time, certain features of the story have been overlooked when such a positive assessment of the story has been reached too quickly and too simplistically. These potentially negative features have created many ethical and theological difficulties for some modern readers; some have even been led to challenge the usability of this story in contemporary communities of faith. The major difficulties along the way to an eventually more positive assessment will be presented briefly in the Introduction and elaborated in more detail at appropriate points in the commentary itself.

Difficulties with the story are not limited to theological and ethical issues, however. They begin with debates over such classic topics as date of composition, purpose, and authorship. The presentation of these matters will be relatively brief, since they are informative but not finally decisive for assessing the theological significance of the story.

Date and Purpose

Ruth is set by its opening line in the era of the Judges and concludes with mention of King David. The composition therefore must be from the time of David or later. Critical scholarship in the first half of the twentieth century proposed that the book was from the era of Ezra and Nehemiah, some 550 years after the reign of David. The arguments for this late date rested primarily on linguistic and grammatical features, such as expressions that appear to show the influence of the Aramaic

1

language upon the Hebrew of Ruth, influences that were thought to be possible only in the post-exilic period as Aramaic became the dominant language of the region. The period of Ezra-Nehemiah was identified as the probable setting because the book looked favorably upon marriage between an Israelite man and a Moabite woman. The viewpoint expressed in Ruth was interpreted as a polemic against the policies of Ezra and Nehemiah that required Jewish men to divorce their non-Jewish wives (cf. Ezra 9–10, Nehemiah 10:28–30; 13:3, 23–30). A post-exilic date was further supported by the author's need to explain an old custom (Ruth 4:7) and by differences between Ruth and earlier legal texts in their approaches to marriage and redemption rights.

A major challenge to this late dating of the book was mounted in 1975 by Edward F. Campbell Jr., who proposed a time frame from about 950–700 B.C.E. (p. 24). Campbell challenged the accuracy of many of the supposed late linguistic and grammatical features and suggested that the closest parallels in literary style were to early stories such as those in the Joseph story of Genesis or the Court History of David in II Samuel. He suggested further that the tone of the book precluded its serving as a polemic against the actions of Ezra and Nehemiah. Rather, the purpose of the story in his view was to entertain and to instruct, to "look at ordinary events as being the scene of God's subtly providential activity" (p. 5).

Since the publication of Campbell's work, debate over the date and purpose of Ruth has been lively. Several studies have reassessed the linguistic features of the book, and additional theories have been proposed that associate the writing with varying political agendas, most often the reinforcement of the prerogatives of the Davidic monarchy. Kirsten Nielsen's 1997 commentary follows this hypothesis about the purpose of the book, arguing that it was originally written to "champion the right of David's family to the throne" (p. 29) and that this purpose could not be relevant to a post-exilic context. Underlying this argument are two assumptions: (1) that late linguistic features are not present and (2) that the prominence of David in the book points to its composition as a defense against critics who were using his known Moabite ancestry in a smear campaign against him or his descendants. This proposal about the purpose of the book still leaves open a variety of occasions known from the pre-exilic period: the initial establishment of David's rule, the era of succession disputes near the end of his life, the controversy with Jeroboam I that led to division of the kingdom, or the reigns of Hezekiah or Josiah, who sought to incorporate northerners into the Judean fold.

The study of linguistic features has been taken up most recently in the 1996 commentary of Frederic W. Bush, who builds upon the recent work of several scholars (Polzin, Hurwitz, Rooker) who have attempted to distinguish "Standard Biblical Hebrew" from "Late Biblical Hebrew." Bush notes that even if the concentration of late forms in 4:7 (which many regard as an interpolation) is discounted, there remain significant examples of features generally associated with writings from the post-exilic period. Overall, he finds in Ruth enough late features to suggest to him a date "later rather than earlier, . . . at the beginning of the post-exilic period" (p. 30). The validity of any such argument depends, of course, upon agreement about the dating of the biblical materials used as the bases for comparison. While agreement on Chronicles, Ezra and Nehemiah, and Esther as post-exilic is easy to reach, there is substantial disagreement today about the relative antiquity of much of the remaining corpus of narrative texts. Although linguistic features seem less subject to bias than proposed purposes of a composition as a basis for dating, it is important to realize that even the discussion of linguistic development is not free of underlying assumptions. This commentary dates the received Hebrew text no earlier than the late pre-exilic period, and quite possibly well into the exilic or even post-exilic period.

Whether the original purpose of the story was to defend the claims of the Davidic line against its detractors also remains open to question. It is true that the book does point to David, by its mention of Ephrathah in the opening verses (1:2; see commentary) and at its end (4:11), as well as by the dual mention of David in the narrative conclusion (4:17) and in the longer statement of his genealogy (4:18–22). Yet it seems unlikely that critics who questioned the legitimacy of the Davidic monarchy because of David's alleged Moabite ancestry would find the personal qualities of his great-grandmother a convincing rebuttal. Furthermore, the antiquity of the genealogy is much disputed, and there is no compelling evidence that it is historically based. Aside from the report that David once left his parents in the care of the king of Moab (I Sam. 22:3–4), there is no reference to any Moabite connection, much less ancestry, in the story of David's rise to power, reign, and succession disputes. Some scholars have explained the oddity of the notice in I Samuel by presuming the historicity of David's Moabite genealogy as attested in Ruth, but such an assumption is speculative at best. It is equally likely that this isolated notice inspired the development of the genealogical tradition at a much later time.

The direction of possible literary dependence between the concluding genealogy in Ruth and the parallel information in I Chronicles 2 is also a matter of dispute, and some scholars would argue that each version is based independently on some underlying source. Whatever the solution to this question, it is clear that the particular form of the genealogy preserved in Ruth is highly stylized. Boaz holds the seventh position, one of special note in traditional genealogies, and David holds the tenth and last position, perhaps also numerically significant. The number of names is certainly insufficient to cover the time-frame from Perez to David in the biblical tradition. Within the genealogy, the names Ram and Salmon are highly problematic, lacking other attestation beyond the parallel in I Chronicles and not spelled consistently even within the Hebrew Bible, much less in the versions. Oddly, the genealogy begins with Perez rather than with his father Judah (the eponymous ancestor of the tribe of Judah); if one posits with Nielsen that writers in the royal court prepared this genealogy for propagandistic purposes, one wonders why they did not begin with Judah (who is also named in the text of Ruth, 4:12) and omit the unknown Ram or Salmon, thus preserving the seventh and tenth places for Boaz and David. Certainly the issues surrounding the genealogy are more complex than can be elaborated here. Again, the point to be underscored is that the details of the genealogy can be understood more readily on the supposition that the story as a whole presumes public acceptance of David's legitimacy than on the supposition that it is designed to defend his legitimacy against detractors.

This commentary therefore takes as its starting point the primary alternative suggested by many commentators from the rabbis onward: an emphasis on instruction concerning the community's view of outsiders. David is foregrounded as the storyteller's means of legitimizing an inclusive attitude towards foreigners, perhaps especially toward foreign women. Even if it had lacked any reference at all to David, the story would still have been effective as entertainment and for teaching the importance of faithful concern for others beyond the call of duty. Ruth's concern for Naomi becomes a model for Boaz's eventual concern for Ruth. This theme of care for others is on the one hand heightened because of Ruth's Moabite ancestry; yet on the other hand, her outsider ancestry could lead those with an exclusivistic, in-group focused perspective to question the very point of the story. This same debate about the limits of neighborliness is raised in the question put to Jesus, "And who is my neighbor?" (Luke 10:29), to which Jesus responded with the story of the Good Samaritan. Who can be counted as faithful, and how far should the boundaries for exercising faithful concern extend? For ancient readers of Ruth who recognized and revered the legitimacy of David's kingship, the references to David would function as an imprimatur, making its controversial claim binding upon

4

them: they should recognize gifts of care and concern from outsiders, and they should extend their own care and concern beyond the boundaries of the bloodline of the covenant community.

Although, as suggested above, an emphasis on challenging the limitations of traditional ethnic barriers might have had special relevance in the era of Ezra and Nehemiah, it is not necessary that the story be composed only at such a late date in order to bear the didactic intent of a word about inclusion. Within the linguistic parameters proposed by Bush, the story could have been read as a challenge to community purity perspectives of the late pre-exilic Deuteronomistic History, with its emphasis against relationships with the local Canaanites. Or it might have addressed in story form the tensions arising already early in the post-exilic era between Jewish returnees from Babylon and those who had remained in the land after the fall of Jerusalem. Noting the repeated need to challenge narrow exclusivism in the life of the ancient community should remind readers that the story of Ruth addresses a perennial issue in the human community.

Authorship

Given the uncertainty about dating the composition of Ruth, authorship can hardly be determined. Jewish tradition attributed the book to the prophet Samuel. In recent decades, the possibility of a woman author has been explored. Van Dijk-Hemmes, in particular, has hypothesized that at least in a stage of oral transmission the story of Ruth may have been passed on by a guild of women storytellers. She identifies three features of the story that might suggest female authorship: (1) "an intent which is less than normally androcentric"; (2) "a (re)definition of reality from the female perspective"; and (3) "defineable [sic] differences between the view of the male and the female figures" (p. 136). The first of these criteria she finds in the motif of cooperation (rather than competition) among women, the second and third criteria in Naomi's reference to mothers' houses (1:8) and in the focus on sons as protection for women (rather than as perpetuators of male lineage, cf. 4:11–12) in 1:11 and 4:15.

Although such arguments for placing this story in the mouths of women are not implausible, no definitive answer to the question of authorial gender can be established. In every culture there are some women who identify primarily with male perspectives and some men who identify primarily with female perspectives. Thus the presence of female perspectives is not, as van Dijk-Hemmes clearly recognizes, an immutable criterion. Yet it is important not to rule out in principle female authorship of this story, whether in an oral telling or even in its preserved written form.   5

Traditions and Customs Underlying the Story

Any ancient story presumes rather than explains many cultural realities that were well understood by its original audience, and Ruth is no exception. Scholars wishing to understand those cultural realities in the service of better understanding of the story itself must look to evidence from other texts of the period, whether within the Bible or from the surrounding cultures. The rules governing the practice of gleaning (Ruth's activity in chapter 2), for instance, are relatively clear from legislation in the books of Leviticus and Deuteronomy; yet certain unspecified details, such as whether the gleaner must gain specific permission from the land owner, have generated technical debates about the interpretation of Ruth's activity. Much more ink has been spilled in scholarly efforts to comprehend Israelite practices of levirate marriage and of land redemption, to determine in what ways these two sets of practices (or traditions or customs or laws) are related to each other, and to decide the applicability of either or both to an interpretation of the story of Ruth.

Regarding levirate marriage, the debate is so extensive and the evidence so complex that many commentaries devote to it either a lengthy section of the introduction or a major excursus (usually located somewhere within chapter 3 or chapter 4). In brief, the custom of levirate marriage provides that a male relative take the responsibility for impregnating a widow whose husband died without leaving male offspring. The rare references to the practice (only one legal text, Deuteronomy 25:5–10, and one narrative, Genesis 38), however, leave many details unclear and in fact do not fully cohere with each other, so it is difficult to know whether the general concept is applicable to the circumstances in Ruth. Some commentators take this practice as basic to the interpretation of the book, while others find that it has no relevance. A bare beginning of the list of questions includes the degree of closeness or distance of blood relation to which the rule applies, whether the rule provides an opportunity (privilege) or an obligation (duty) for the widow, and whether the rule applies beyond the bounds of the Israelite community.

Within the story of Ruth, the possible relevance of such a practice arises initially with Naomi's lament (1:12–13) that she cannot give birth to more sons who could become future husbands for Ruth and Orpah. The conversation between Ruth and Boaz at the threshing floor (chapter 3) and the subsequent exchange between Boaz and the nearer kinsman at the town gate (chapter 4) raise the issue in a more acute manner. Neither Boaz nor the nearer kinsman fits readily within the scope of levirate kinship seen in the other biblical texts. Although there is reference to preserving the name of the dead man (4:5, 10), Boaz (not Elimelech or Mahlon) is named as the father of the child.

With respect to the system of land redemption and the role of the redeemer (Hebrew *gō'ēl*), comparable difficulties arise in interpreting chapters 3 and 4. How is it that Boaz can speak of Naomi's selling a piece of land, when she is portrayed as a destitute widow? Why is he in charge of the transaction? How is the ownership of the land connected with a marriage to Ruth? Whether the Hebrew term for redeemer was ever linked with levirate marriage practice, or whether it was confined strictly to the economic realm, such as in redemption of property belonging to a destitute relative, remains in dispute. Since marriage and redemption vocabulary both appear in Ruth, and since the debate over levirate practice is still unresolved, the confusion is greatly compounded.

Readers interested in pursuing these difficult topics in technical detail are referred to Bush's extensive treatment (pp. 166–69, 199–239). Here a much briefer assessment of the problems, in many respects following Bush's proposal, has been incorporated into the commentary at appropriate points. The starting assumption is that the story would have made sense to its earliest hearers, so that features that appear awkward or inconsistent or mysterious to us would have been at least relatively clear to those who lived in the culture of the storyteller. Since that culture did change over time (as signaled by the narrator's explanatory note about practices of "former times" in 4:7), the interpretation focuses on a reconstruction that makes sense within the structure of this particular narrative, without trying to force the story into the confines of related texts on the theme of levirate marriage. Broadly summarized, the commentary supposes that in 4:3–6, land redemption represents a legal right as well as an obligation, whereas marriage to Ruth represents a moral (but not legal) obligation. Similarly, Naomi's words to her daughters-in-law in 1:11–13 focus on Ruth and Orpah's welfare, not on the preservation of a male line. In both cases, speech using motifs from the practice of levirate marriage is used for a different purpose.

Canonical Context

In the Hebrew Bible, the book of Ruth is found in the third section of the canon, traditionally designated "The Writings." Ruth is part of a set of five "Festival Scrolls" (*Megillot*) designated for reading on the major holy days of the Jewish calendar. (The others are Song of Songs, Ecclesiastes, Lamentations, Esther.) The book is read at the Feast of Weeks (roughly the time of the Christian Pentecost celebration) because of its association with the harvest season (cf. Lev. 23:15–21; Num. 28:26–31). While the tradition of placing Ruth among the Writings is attested as early as the first century C.E., the sub-collection of the five festival scrolls as a group apparently took place several centuries later. The order of these five scrolls varies among manuscripts. An order based on the calendrical sequence of festivals is attested, as is also an order based on the place of each book in the chronology of Israel's history. In this latter ordering, Ruth appears first because of its association with King David.

The location of the book of Ruth in Christian Bibles follows the Greek and Latin manuscript tradition in placing the story after the book of Judges, as suggested by the opening line of the story, "In the days when the judges ruled . . . " This location is also attested very early and probably goes back to another strand of Jewish tradition in the Greco-Roman period. The chronological context of the era of the Judges, which would certainly be apparent to readers regardless of the canonical location of the book itself, is suggestive for the interpretation of the book. Judges and Ruth offer a study in contrasts (see comment on 1:1). Judges features warfare, violence, and repeated instances of Israel's disobedience; Ruth features a peaceful village, orderly public process, and a faithful foreigner who directs an Israelite toward a higher path of justice and generosity. More specifically, the book of Judges ends with escalation of intertribal warfare. After the assembled Israelite tribes go to battle against one of their own and kill off all members of their brother tribe of Benjamin except for six hundred men, the victors suddenly become anxious that the Benjaminite tribe will be "cut off" (Judges 21:6) without progeny. Their solution to obtaining suitable wives for these six hundred Benjaminites requires further wholesale killing, followed by mass kidnapping. The need to preserve a family line is accomplished only by an outpouring of violence. In the story of Ruth, the theme of preserving a family line also appears (cf. 4:5, 10), this time for lack of men rather than women. Here, however, the problem is resolved not by murder and mayhem, but through the bold and caring action of a woman (who may actually be less concerned for family name; see above on traditions and customs) and the upright response of a leading male citizen who makes a moral choice to go beyond the minimum requirements of legal duty and beyond the usual boundaries of acceptable choices for marriage partners.

Beyond the context of the era of the Judges, the story of Ruth reaches back to the story of the birth of Perez (Genesis 38; cf. Ruth 4:12, 18). Indeed the storyteller looks back even further, to Rachel and Leah (4:11), thus giving Ruth a place of honor alongside the classic mothers of Israel. Reaching ahead, the story connects with King David (indirectly in 1:1–2; directly in 4:17, 18–22). The genealogy that closes the book is presented also in a more segmented format in I Chronicles 2:5–16. Each of these connections is addressed at appropriate points in the commentary.

Despite these multiple direct and indirect allusions to other parts of the Old Testament canon, no Old Testament text outside the book of Ruth makes reference to this story. The one external reference within the Christian canon appears in the opening genealogy of the Gospel according to Matthew (1:5). Here Ruth is one of four women (alongside Tamar mother of Perez, Rahab, and the "wife of Uriah") who are included in a list of forty-two generations of male ancestors of "Joseph the husband of Mary, of whom Jesus was born" (Matt. 1:16). Scholars are unanimous in supposing that these four women were not selected at random, but there is considerable diversity of opinion about the principle(s) of selection at work. Three of the women named are presumed in Old Testament tradition to be non-Israelite (Gentiles); the fourth, Tamar, is regarded as non-Israelite in later Jewish tradition. All four women's stories refer to sexual activity and/or marriage circumstances that would normally be regarded as unacceptable; but Rahab's involvement is only in her occupation as prostitute while hiding the Israelite spies (Joshua 2:1), not with regard to her own place in the genealogy. Although Matthew's identification of the Canaanite Rahab as Boaz's mother might be used to explain Boaz's more positive attitude toward the non-Israelite Ruth, there is in fact no mention of Rahab as Boaz's mother anywhere in any extant Jewish tradition. The Matthean genealogy may have included Rahab by extrapolation from a documented tradition that Rahab was a proselyte member of the tribe of Judah (Johnson, pp. 162–65), but this connection still has nothing to do with irregular sexual activity. Thus all four women cannot be fitted neatly into either the category of Gentiles or the category of questionable sexual encounters with the fathers of their offspring. Still, the names of these women may anticipate Matthew's interest in including Gentiles and possibly may hint that Jesus' unusual birth was not a disqualification from messiahship. It may be more instructive, however, not to focus narrowly on their ethnicity or their sexuality, but rather to take account of the overall stories of these women: "none of them fits in with the way things are 'supposed' to be" (Gaventa, p. 38). In this way Ruth and the others prepare the way for Mary, whose pregnancy by the Holy Spirit and whose child who will persistently challenge the status quo certainly do not "fit," even though the work is of God.

Theological Themes
1. The Peaceable Community

Beginning with famine and death, the story of Ruth ends with community harvest and rejoicing over the birth of a baby. The narrator's portrait of Bethlehem in the concluding scenes in chapter 4 offers a vision of

9

a harmonious and joyful community. Boaz ensures that all matters are handled decently and in order; there is uprightness in the meeting at the town gate. The leading man of the Israelite village and the poor Moabite widow are married with the blessing of the community elders and others gathered round. The child of this union is celebrated by the women of the town as he is placed into the arms of Naomi. The continuing bond between Ruth and Naomi is underscored as the women compare Ruth's value to that of seven sons. This portrait of the community may be regarded as a microcosm of the peaceable kingdom envisioned by the prophetic tradition. It is a human community in which the marginalized person has dared to insist upon full participation, in which the one in the center has reached out beyond societal norms to include the marginalized. It is a community in which children are celebrated and the elderly are attentively cared for. It is a community in which all are fed, a community in which joy is the dominant note. Thus the story offers to its readers "a memory of the future" (Russell, p. 27), a vision of future hope couched in the form of a story from the past.

This view of the story has been challenged in recent years from various perspectives by both lay and scholarly interpreters, especially by those concerned for a feminist hermeneutic of suspicion. First and foremost, it has been pointed out that the long-term economic security of women in this story is dependent upon the marriage of one of them to a wealthy man. This approach to economic security, it is rightly argued, is not structurally adequate to the full humanity of women as it is understood at the turn of the millennium, at least in most western cultures. Others point to the celebration of a boy child and the reference to Rachel and Leah (4:11) as indicators that the narrative implicitly devalues girls. Still others express concern over the role given to Naomi in relation to the baby (4:16–17), fearing a basis for reinscribing customs in which mothers' roles are denigrated in favor of a grandmother's authority.

These and similar objections put to the story serve as important reminders that the story is not without problems, that it is not so idyllic in every respect that its portrait of future hope can be accepted without critical reflection. At the same time, however, one must be careful not to throw out the proverbial baby with the bath water. Given that Israelite society gave preference to men in many spheres of life, it is to be expected that biblical texts will carry that explicit or implicit bias in their very warp and woof. In every instance, therefore, faithful readers must choose which aspects of the text they find authoritative, and which aspects they will not seek to preserve in their own cultures and societal structures. It is scarcely likely, for instance, that modern Western readers will think of replicating in their own community decision-making the exact procedures used at the town gate, particularly the system of sealing decisions by removal of a shoe. Which parts of a text should be literally replicated must be considered again and again by successive communities of faith. The more enduring and underlying principles of a peaceable community—inclusion of the stranger, basic and continuing sustenance, respect for all ages and both genders—represented by the story have been embodied in many ways by different communities through the centuries, and conversation about how to do that better will surely continue. In assessing the significance of Ruth for this conversation, it is essential to read the story as one individual picture of the true meaning of human community, rather than as a prescription for how that community ought always to be organized.

2. Examples of Loyal Living

The story of Ruth portrays not only an instance of the peaceable community, but also examples or models of ways of human interaction that foster the coming into being of such community. Each of the principal characters—Ruth, Boaz, and to a lesser extent Naomi—chooses to act in ways that promote the well-being of others. The praise accorded to Ruth and Boaz, validating their actions and choices, lies generally on the lips of other characters in the story, rather than in the words of the narrator. Ruth is praised by Boaz (2:11–12; 3:10) and by the women of Bethlehem (4:15). Boaz is praised indirectly by Naomi (2:19–20, see comment), by Ruth (3:17), and by the townspeople who pray for his marriage (4:11–12).

It is notable that the minor characters—Orpah and the nearer kinsman who appear briefly and just as quickly leave the stage—are not criticized for their behavior. It is as if they do what is expected in the context of the story, not less but not more, nothing requiring reprimand, yet nothing worthy of praise, whether from the narrator or from other participants. Thus it is the extraordinary behavior of Ruth in response to Naomi's need, together with the extraordinary behavior of Boaz in response to Ruth's example and suggestion, that moves the story from grief to joy, from emptiness to fullness.

The Hebrew term for the kind of extraordinary behavior witnessed in this story is *ḥesed,* usually translated "kindness" or "loyalty" in the NRSV. The Hebrew term is a strong one. It refers to care or concern for another with whom one is in relationship, but care that specifically takes shape in action to rescue the other from a situation of desperate need, and under circumstances in which the rescuer is uniquely qualified to

11

do what is needed. Thus Ruth's determination to accompany Naomi on the journey from Moab to Bethlehem, to cast her lot with an older woman rather than to seek her own welfare in her homeland, goes beyond normal expectations of their relationship. Ruth's continuing care in seeking food for the despairing Naomi and her willingness to cooperate in the risky visit to the threshing floor are recognized by Boaz as evidence of this special category of extraordinary commitment. Boaz, for his part, responds by making special provision for Ruth to receive generous gleanings and by agreeing readily to pursue the arrangement for marriage suggested to him by Ruth at the threshing floor; his actions benefit Naomi as well as Ruth. Naomi, despite her sense of hopelessness at the loss of her husband and sons, offered a plan for the security and happiness of her daughters-in-law (1:8–9). This initial plan of course came to nought in Ruth's case when Ruth refused to return to her Moabite family. Once in Bethlehem, Naomi seems overwhelmed at first by her sense of bitterness and emptiness, sure that God has abandoned her. Yet, after the turning point where she connects Boaz's generosity with God's hand (2:20; see commentary), she shows renewed concern for Ruth (2:22), and at the end of the harvest season she initiates a new plan to ensure Ruth's future (3:1).

Here we have a story of two women working together to make a way out of no way, to find security in the midst of a system that has little to offer to widows without families. First one woman, then the other, as the occasion arises, takes initiative to set their course. The significance of this example of solidarity among women is heightened because of their different ages, their ethnic backgrounds from groups traditionally at enmity with one another, and their specific relationship as mother-in-law to daughter-in-law, a relationship regarded by many cultures as potentially filled with tension and even discord. For the sake of this relationship Ruth is determined to make her way in a potentially hostile environment. That determination in turn is given an entry point by the openness of Boaz, whose example as community leader appears in the end to win over any opposition in the Bethlehemite community.

Just as a feminist hermeneutic of suspicion has challenged the story's concluding vision of a peaceable community (see above), so also that hermeneutic has challenged interpretations of the story that emphasize the altruistic caring exhibited by its chief characters. Fewell and Gunn in particular have argued that the actions of each character can just as easily be seen as self-serving, motivated by personal interests rather than the interests of the other. To achieve this result, Fewell and Gunn read many of the quotations attributed to the various characters as masking hidden motives. Many speeches are intended not as

12

expressions of true feelings, but rather as rhetorical ploys to gain the acquiescence or cooperation of the other. When Naomi, for example, says to Ruth that she needs to seek security for Ruth (3:1), she is supposed actually to be thinking of her own security but choosing her words to evoke Ruth's cooperation. Ruth's famous words of commitment to Naomi (1:16–17) do indicate to Naomi that Ruth will not be deterred; but it is suggested that Ruth will go to any length to avoid returning to her Moabite family, so that she speaks not from true conviction but primarily to silence Naomi's objections by sheer force of argument.

Such alternative readings do call attention to gaps in the text that are not explicitly clarified by the narrator and that may be unthinkingly filled by the interpreter. Such readings also serve to remind readers that nearly every action taken by a human being can be interpreted psychologically as involving a mixture of motives. Nonetheless, a more traditional reading that takes seriously the basic theme of caring and responsibility for others makes more sense of the story as a whole and fits better with the general style of Hebrew narrative, where dialogue not meant to be taken at face value is typically so marked by the narrator or by other characters.

A literary and rhetorical argument for such an altruistic interpretation of the characters' motives does not, however, do away with the feminist objection that this story, and especially Ruth's behavior, encourages women to follow cultural expectations by serving others at the expense of their own needs, by sacrificing themselves for the sake of family or friends or workplace colleagues. The danger of such an interpretation may be especially acute in some Asian cultures, where some church leaders are reported to have used the example of Ruth to insist that young Christian women maintain a traditional cultural practice of serving their mothers-in-law rather than choosing to live as a nuclear family or to work outside the home. Comparable use of scripture in support of unreflective self-sacrifice is familiar to many women in many cultures and in many spheres of life beyond the family.

Numerous factors in the story, however, suggest that the concern Ruth shows for others belongs to the category of appropriate caring rather than unthinking self-sacrifice. First, concern for others is expressed by many characters, *not just by Ruth, not just by women.* Naomi and the women of Bethlehem, as well as Boaz and the men of Bethlehem, join Ruth in expressions of concern. Boaz's role is of special note, since his caring actions as a powerful male often parallel or mirror Ruth's. Second, Ruth makes her own *choice* to follow Naomi; in so doing she in fact rejects Naomi's advice. The circumstances of chapter 1 are so unusual (see commentary) that probably even the ancient hearers of the story were not sure about a "normal" or "customary" choice in such a situation. Third, this is a story about basic *survival*, shorter-term and long-term economic survival. That one person should commit to another in such a context is far removed from being used as a doormat or refusing an opportunity for self-actualization. Fourth, the story is about *women's* survival. By turn Ruth and Naomi are supporting one another. Their concern is for their survival as women, not for preservation of a male lineage system (see commentary on 1:11–14 and 4:14–17). Finally, both Ruth and Naomi make choices in which their efforts become mutually beneficial. Survival for one woman means survival for both. This potential for mutuality and its result is especially evident in the threshing floor sequence (see commentary on chapter 3). A relationship that began in tension moves toward *solidarity*. With such safeguards in place in the story itself, an altruistic interpretation of the characters supports rather than undermines the full humanity of women.

3. The Place of God in the Story

A key feature of the book is its effort to relate human care and concern to divine care and concern in the working out of human difficulties and pain along the road to the peaceable community. Here God does not have a speaking role; on the other hand God is not so absent from the story as in the Hebrew version of Esther, where the name of God does not even appear. Nor is God completely behind the scenes, as in the Joseph narrative. In Ruth, the narrator reports two direct interventions by God into the human affairs of the story. The latter of these is stated quite directly: "the LORD made [Ruth] conceive" (4:13), thus bringing an end to her implicit period of barrenness during her marriage to Mahlon. The earlier intervention of God is stated somewhat less directly: Naomi "had heard . . . that the LORD had considered his people and given them food" (1:6). Nonetheless, the gift of food is reported in the words of the narrator, thus representing fact. These two interventions, the giving of food and of pregnancy, represent areas of life over which ancient Israelites experienced little sense of human control. Elsewhere, the direction of the story of Ruth could be and indeed was determined largely by human decision, as suggested above; but the deity's two interventions set the parameters of the story. From a literary perspective, the introductory verses quickly set up the dual problems of famine and of the death of the males of Naomi's family without offspring (1:1–5). God's direct actions then bracket the remainder of the story with its focus on human resolution.

Yet God is mentioned repeatedly in the words of the various char-

14

acters, most often in their prayers, sometimes in other contexts. The first such instance appears in Naomi's words of farewell blessing upon her daughters-in-law (1:9). Naomi, unable to help Ruth and Orpah find husbands, commends them and their need to God's faithful care. Subsequently, Ruth commits herself to Naomi's God (1:16), although the personal name Yahweh (the LORD) does not appear here. Upon arriving in Bethlehem, Naomi speaks of God as she expresses her despair (1:20–21), reiterating the theme expressed to her daughters-in-law at 1:13. Four times she expresses the pain of her experience of abandonment by God, with no hint of expectation that this (perceived) condition will change. Although Naomi speaks here in terms of direct divine intervention, it should be noted that her words are actually her interpretive claims, not "facts" stated by the narrator. Within the design of the narrative, Naomi's bitterness over God's treatment of her will be undone by unfolding events through which she will discover that God has not after all abandoned her (2:20).

When Boaz first meets Ruth, he prays for her "full reward from the LORD" (2:12). His prayer thus joins with Naomi's earlier petition that the LORD deal kindly with Ruth; but as yet the means for fulfilling of these prayers is not in view. As Ruth returns from the field and reports where she has gleaned, Naomi invokes the LORD's blessing on Boaz (2:20). This verse represents the turning point in the story (see commentary), as the first hint of how the prayers for Ruth are fulfilled appears on the horizon. The action of God does not take the form of direct intervention, but happens through the actions of the human characters. Naomi's invoking of this blessing also represents the turning point in her journey out of despair and passivity; indeed it is her initiative that will pave the way for Boaz's action (3:1–4). Both Naomi and Boaz themselves bring to fruition the prayers they have made to God on Ruth's behalf.

Twice more God's name appears in the text, first in prayers led by the elders of the community for Ruth's fertility in the upcoming marriage (4:11), then in the blessing (praise) of God by the women of the community for the baby boy and faithful daughter-in-law who make an end of the emptiness in Naomi's life (4:14–15). In the course of events, no one has prayed overtly for Naomi. But Ruth's loyalty to her from beginning to end has created conditions whereby Naomi's sorrow is turned to celebration.

Thus within the broad parameters of the gifts of daily bread and of human life itself, the book of Ruth presents God's working as hidden and mysterious, like yeast at work in a loaf of bread, until all is transformed. God is at work through the everyday actions of faithful people

15

seeking to manifest divine loyalty in their loyal interactions with those around them. To be sure, readers are not to shrink from attributing blessings in their lives to the work of God; indeed they should join the participants in the story of Ruth in praising and thanking God for those gifts. But at the same time, readers are invited to look for the human component in the blessings they receive, and, like Ruth especially, to live in such a way that their own actions become the channel for God's blessings upon those around them.

PART ONE

From Judah to Moab and Return

RUTH 1

Ruth 1:1–5
Prologue

The story of Ruth opens with a condensed introduction of basic information, the kind that modern readers might easily pass over in their rush to get to the main action. Yet each component of the introduction is critical to an appreciation of the story that is to unfold.

"In the days when the judges ruled" provides specificity to the once-upon-a-time character of the tale to be told. In English Bibles, the story of Ruth is placed in its appropriate chronological context, immediately after the book of Judges. Although in the Hebrew Bible the story is gathered together with other festival scrolls (see Introduction), readers in the Jewish tradition have certainly also recognized the significance of its chronological setting. The book of Judges presents this era as one of repeated bloody battles between Israel and its Canaanite, Philistine, and other enemies, as well as of warfare among various Israelite tribes. It is also a time of repeated disobedience to God's covenant stipulations, a time marked by a struggle to learn how to be faithful to God in the new setting of the promised land. The book of Judges concludes with a concern for the survival of the Benjaminite tribe, of whom only men are left alive; women are secured for these surviving men by intertribal warfare and by kidnapping. Then the narrator concludes the book as a whole: "In those days there was no king in Israel; all the people did what was right in their own eyes" (Judges 21:25). The implication is that the absence of centralized, hereditary leadership contributed to the wrongdoing of the people.

The entire story in the book of Ruth serves as counterpoint to this picture of the era of the Judges. It moves from the tribal level to the familial; it moves from warfare to constructive and peaceful individual action; it provides examples of faithful obedience, doing justice, loving mercy, and walking attentively with God (Micah 6:8). Upright action by both Israelite and foreigner is displayed by contrast to the wrongdoing of the people in Judges. And this upright action sets in motion the emergence of the royal leadership whose absence is lamented by the concluding line of Judges. This counterpoint is heightened by the location "Bethlehem in Judah," since two of the stories of violence toward the end of Judges open with characters setting out from Bethlehem in Judah (Judges 17; 19).

Having set the time frame with its cultural and theological ramifications, the author now presents the circumstance that sets the entire story in motion: famine in the land. Famine and migration because of famine are well known in the Old Testament tradition. Abraham goes to Egypt because of famine (Gen. 12:10), Isaac goes to Gerar (Gen. 26:1); Joseph's managerial prudence in conserving grain for use during a regional famine leads eventually to the migration of his father and brothers from Canaan to Egypt (Genesis 43). Famine is the implication of some of the traditional covenant curses—drought (Deut. 28:23–24) and insect plague (Deut. 28:38–42). In a subsistence agrarian economy where the quantity of food production is barely adequate on an annual basis, even in a good year, where long-term storage and long-range transport of food are not practical realities, the prospect of famine was and still is terrifying. Contemporary news reports from around the globe serve as reminder that famine is not just a bygone terror; every year peoples migrate in search of food or starve and become victims of disease because they are unable to migrate or find other sources of food.

Thus readers should not be surprised that one Israelite man decides to migrate before it is too late. He is apparently an ordinary citizen; the narrator provides only his name, Elimelech, and the names of his wife and two sons. Yet the name of his hometown strikes a chord, both of dissonance and of anticipation, once the whole story is known. In Hebrew, "Bethlehem" means literally "house of bread" or "house of food," so there is an immediate irony in the name of the man's town, an irony that highlights the severity of the famine: even in "House of Bread" there was apparently no food, no prospect for food. At the same time, the reader familiar with the story of David, to be told in I–II Samuel, recognizes that Bethlehem of Judah is David's town (I Samuel 16) and will think ahead to the genealogy of David that concludes the story of Ruth. As Judges ends with the notation that there was no king in Israel, so Ruth ends with the name of David, who will institute God's divinely chosen dynasty ruling over Judah.

From Bethlehem, "house of bread/food" where there is no food, the man of Bethlehem migrates to Moab, across the Jordan River to the east of Bethlehem. Why the family goes to Moab rather than somewhere else is not explained. The climate of Moab varies from area to area, as does the climate in the land presumed to be occupied by Israel in the time of the Judges. The author refers regularly to the "country" of Moab (1:1, 2, 6, 22; 2:6; 4:3); possibly this phrase represents a specific sub-region of Moabite territory, but what area is involved can no longer be determined. It is possible that some region of Moab might not have been affected as severely by a given drought as the region around Bethlehem. Yet since the text claims that the famine encompassed "the land," a much broader area than Bethlehem, a significant difference in circumstances in Moab is more difficult to explain.

Although the ancient hearers of the story may or may not have regarded Moab as a sensible place for a famine-stricken family to search for food, the wider biblical context makes clear that Moab would have been regarded as an undesirable destination on other grounds. Although there are some positive references to Moab, the larger picture is generally negative. Tradition remembered that Israelite men became sexually involved with Moabite women and that apostasy resulted from that involvement (Num. 25:1–2). The king of Moab hired the diviner Balaam to curse Israel and destroy them (Numbers 22–24); only God's intervention caused Balaam to bless Israel rather than curse them. Moab was among the oppressors of Israel in the era of the Judges (Judges 3:12ff). Deuteronomy 23:3 forbids the presence of Moabites in the Israelite religious assembly; in the time of Nehemiah this law became the basis for separating from Israel "all those of foreign descent" (Neh. 13:1). Although neither the date of composition of Ruth nor the dates of these other traditions can be determined with certainty, the evidence points to Israel's long-standing negative view of Moab and its people, and this perspective forms the backdrop for all that transpires in the story of Ruth: the deaths of the men of the family, the magnitude of Ruth's decision to accompany Naomi, the negative attitude of the field workers toward Ruth, the refusal of the nearer redeemer to marry Ruth, the contrasting favorable attitude of Boaz toward Ruth, and the portrait of a Moabite woman as one who acts faithfully and loyally.

Some scholars have argued that both the possibility of food and a positive view of Moab would be required in order for the story to have plausibility for the ancient hearer. But that is not necessarily the case. The author may equally or even more probably have wanted hearers to be taken aback and thus drawn in by the very oddity of Elimelech's choice of destination. A reader or hearer is even more quickly drawn in when the story's character makes an improbable decision or takes improbable action in the very first line. The likelihood that the narrative presumes Moab to be an implausible destination is underscored by the continuing series of improbable turns of event as the story proceeds.

Having established this theologically evocative setting in time and place, the author introduces the names of the characters and something of their origin. Although many names of biblical characters have meanings, the meanings of the names in this story are not clear. It has been noted that the names of the two sons Mahlon and Chilion rhyme, a feature sometimes found in folk-tales. The name Naomi may refer to sweetness or pleasantness (by contrast to her request in 1:20 to be called Mara, which means "bitter"). The phrase "Bethlehem in Judah" appears for the second time, as specification of the origin of this Ephrathite family. The term Ephrathite has varying uses in the Old Testament, sometimes identifying persons from the area of Ephraim well to the north of Judah. Here it does not have that meaning, but identifies the geographical and/or sub-tribe unit to which Elimelech's family belongs. Its mention serves to heighten the connection of the story with King David, who is described in I Samuel 17:12 as the son of "an Ephrathite of Bethlehem in Judah," the only other occurrence of this phrase apart from Ruth 1:2. In prophetic tradition, Micah 5:2 (Heb. v. 1) anticipates a new and upright ruler from the Davidic line; from Bethlehem of Ephrathah "shall come forth . . . one who is to rule in Israel."

Elimelech dies in Moab, and subtly the narrator brings Naomi to the fore as "she was left with her two sons." The sons marry Moabite women Orpah and Ruth. The sequence of names Orpah and Ruth, with Mahlon mentioned before Chilion in vv. 2 and 5, might suggest that Ruth was married to Chilion; but 4:10 specifies that Ruth was the wife of Mahlon. After ten years, the two sons die as well; again Naomi is the focus of the narrator, although she is not named by name: "the woman" was left bereft of the men of her family. The Hebrew does not make clear whether the ten years' time refers to the entire period beginning with the family's arrival in Moab, or whether the marriages had lasted ten years before the two sons died. In either case, but especially if one assumes ten years of marriage, Ruth is implicitly portrayed as a barren woman in this stage-setting introduction. The narrator's comment toward the end of the story that "the LORD made her conceive" (4:13) suggests that Ruth should be viewed in the line of Sarah, Rachel, Manoah's wife (Judges 13), and Hannah, each of whom bore a child of significance for Israel's story after God removed her barrenness.

20

The narrator offers no explanation, natural or theological, for the death of Elimelech and his sons. Theorizing from the negative biblical view of the Moabites described above, some traditions of interpretation explain Elimelech's death as divine punishment for taking his family to Moabite territory. In the same way, it is suggested that his sons died because they married Moabite wives. While this is certainly a possible interpretation, the narrator's lack of attention to any reason suggests that the answer to the question is not central to the meaning of the story. The deaths of the three men serve to draw our attention to Naomi, whose life up to this point in her culture would have revolved around her husband and sons. What is to become of this Hebrew widow with no male support in a foreign land? As the story unfolds, the question of the foreign land receives an immediate but surprising resolution— Naomi will elect to return home, but accompanied by a Moabite woman. The matter of male support is not resolved until the conclusion of the story.

Ruth 1:6–18
Departure for Bethlehem

The extended presentation of the departure scene is structured by a series of speeches. Two long statements by Naomi are separated by a single sentence spoken by her two daughters-in-law. Then a brief third exhortation by Naomi leads to Ruth's extended reply in verses 16–17, perhaps the best-known lines in the entire book. The unit may thus be divided into three sections: verses 6–10, Naomi's first speech and Ruth and Orpah's initial response; verses 11–14, Naomi's second speech and Ruth and Orpah's second response; verses 15–18: Naomi's final speech and Ruth's response.

First Speech and Response Cycle (1:6–10)

The opening words announce Naomi's departure from Moab; the verb "return" indicates that her destination is Judah, even before this is stated in the following sentence. At first glance, her decision seems to be a consequence of her condition as a woman without husband or sons, since her departure follows immediately upon that description of her. But the statement of her departure in verse 6 sets her action in a larger

21

context. Although we are not told how it happened, word had reached her that "the LORD had considered his people and given them food." The famine in Judah had ended, and it ended not by chance but by God's providential hand. Here is the first mention of the deity in the narrative, and one of only two wherein the narrator describes God as taking direct action to intervene in human circumstances pertinent to this story. The other concerns Ruth's conception (4:13) and creates a narrative bracket as the two problems (famine and barrenness) raised by the story's prologue are addressed by divine intervention at the very beginning and very end of the main narrative.

Although ancient farmers were no doubt well-versed in lore relating to productivity, the typical reasons for crop failure (insect plague or lack of rain) and resultant famine would be beyond their control. Thus the provision of food marking the cessation of famine would be readily thought to require action by God. It has been claimed that Israel's religion was historically oriented, by contrast to the nature and fertility focus of Canaanite and other ancient Near Eastern religious thought and practice. More recently, however, scholars have questioned this sharp dichotomy. Israel's neighbors did believe that their gods participated in the ordering of political life and historical events, and Israel for its part believed that its God controlled the coming of rains, seedtime and harvest. The key difference is that Israel believed that Yahweh alone controlled such events—any other heavenly beings were subordinate and obedient only to Yahweh's commanding power.

The simple statement in Ruth that God gave the people food belongs in the larger biblical framework with poetic images from the psalms depicting God as provider of sustenance for all creation (e.g., Psalm 104), with portraits like that given in Jeremiah of the return from exile as a time of rejoicing over grain, wine, oil, and productive flocks (Jer. 31:12–14), and even with an eschatological picture of plenty such as that of Ezekiel 47 with its ever-bearing fruit trees and fish-filled, fresh-water, no longer "Dead" Sea. And yet the story of Ruth shows us that human action is required before God's gift of food can become realized for particular individuals. Divine provision of potential sustenance is a necessary beginning point, but only a beginning.

As verse 2c seems to resume verse 1 in the opening paragraph of the story, repeating some information already given, so verse 7 resumes verse 6, now indicating that the destination is indeed the land of Judah. We are not told why the daughters-in-law are accompanying Naomi, or how far the three have proceeded on their journey before she addresses them. The customs of Israel concerning family structure in a situation of female in-laws bereft of male family members are not known, nor are the customs of Moab. This lack of knowledge is compounded here by the presence of two ethnic groups in the family, as well as the migration between the two homelands. Thus it is not possible for modern interpreters to know what behavior within this part of the story should be regarded as usual and what as unusual or extraordinary. Perhaps the total configuration of circumstances was so unusual even in ancient Israel that the early hearers of the story did not themselves have a clear picture of what should be regarded as usual and what as exceptional, although Boaz certainly speaks as though he is impressed with Ruth's decision (2:11–12). Thus interpreters of this interchange between Naomi and her daughters-in-law make different, indeed opposite, proposals concerning the tone, motivation, and intent of the actors and their words. Trible and many others see altruism at work here, while Fewell and Gunn read the characters as basically self-interested if not self-serving.

At some point on the journey Naomi apparently concludes that Orpah and Ruth are not just "seeing her off," accompanying her for a part of the journey. Indeed, the wording of verse 7 suggests that all three initially intended to make the entire journey, so perhaps Naomi has second thoughts about the intention of her companions, rather than a fresh realization that they plan to continue with her. However it happens that their journey together reaches this juncture, Naomi speaks words to initiate separation. Her words have three parts: an instruction, a general blessing, and a prayer with specific content.

Instruction (v. 8a): Naomi instructs Ruth and Orpah to go back home, each to her "mother's house." The expression is uncommon in the Hebrew Bible; reference to the "father's house" is much more typical. Indeed, some ancient Greek and Syriac manuscripts have the word for "father" instead of "mother" at this point. Theories about why Naomi uses the uncommon phrase range from the possibility that it is a more delicate and feminine expression, thus suitable for women's speech (Joüon, p. 36), to the recent suggestion of Meyers (pp. 109–14) that the expression appears because the context refers to arrangements for future husbands for the two widowed daughters, as is made explicit in verse 9. Meyers points to the use of "mother's house" in the story of Rebekah (Gen. 24:28) where marriage arrangements are in view, and she raises the possibility that mothers played a far more significant role in the decisions about the selection of husbands than the male-focused biblical tradition would lead one to guess. While our knowledge of the ancient culture is insufficient to be certain about such a proposal, the literary effect of the expression is striking. In proposing to sever the relationship with her daughters-in-law, Naomi chooses an expression that draws attention to women's interconnections (Trible, p. 169).

23

Blessing (v. 8b): Following upon the instruction to return to their mothers' houses, Naomi invokes a farewell blessing upon her two daughters-in-law. She prays that God will "deal kindly" with her daughters-in-law as they have dealt with her. This blessing incorporates the first of a series of uses of the Hebrew term *hesed,* variously translated as kindness, lovingkindness, faithfulness, or loyalty, a term that is of central thematic importance for the book as a whole. In the Hebrew Bible *hesed* refers to an action by one person on behalf of another under circumstances that meet three main criteria. First, the action is essential to the survival or basic well-being of the recipient; it is not a matter of taking care of some casual or frivolous whim or desire. Furthermore, the needed action is one that only the person doing the act of *hesed* is in a position to provide; while it is not impossible that there could be some other provider, none is apparent on the immediate horizon of the situation. Finally, an act of *hesed* takes place or is requested within the context of an existing, established, and positive relationship between the persons involved. It is not done "out of the blue"; it is not done in order to establish a relationship not yet existing; the term is not used to refer to actions in human settings where forgiveness is needed to reestablish a positive relationship between the parties. Thus, contrary to older commentaries and translations, the English term "grace" is not well-suited as an English equivalent for the range of meaning of this Hebrew term (Sakenfeld, *The Meaning of Hesed*).

Ruth 1:8b records Naomi's action when from her point of view she is not in a position to do anything more for the two daughters-in-law with whom she has been in familial relationship for an extended period of time. (Her reasoning in this regard will be made explicit in v. 12.) In the absence of her own ability to act on their behalf, she commits them to God's kindness (*hesed*), to action to be done for them by God. The words she uses may reflect not just a general wish, but a formulaic expression by which to bring a relationship to an end without recrimination or sense of disloyalty on either side. By invoking divine *hesed* on behalf of Ruth and Orpah, Naomi signals to them that they are free of any continuing commitment to her. These words expressing her willing intent to bring the relationship to a close both preempt a negative interpretation of Orpah's choice and set the stage for revealing the depth of Ruth's loyalty (*hesed,* cf. 3:10) in her decision to accompany Naomi.

A similar instance of such "benedictory" invocation of divine faithfulness in the context of concluding a relationship may be found in II Samuel 15:20. King David, in flight from Absalom's insurgency, urges the foreigner Ittai and his men to separate themselves from him and concludes his exhortation with the words "may the LORD show steadfast love (*hesed*) and faithfulness to you." In a situation where he can do no more for his supporter, David releases him from further mutual obligation. Like Naomi, David asks God to give what David can no longer provide; like Ruth, Ittai refuses to lay down the commitment he has undertaken.

In calling for God's kindness on behalf of her daughters-in-law, Naomi alludes to their kindness to her and to the dead men of the family. Their kindness is not so much the reason why God should act as it is a standard of behavior that Naomi calls upon God to emulate. We are not told the precise content of their kindness. Presumably it consisted of many individual acts that could be summarized as their loyal state of being with regard to this family of foreigners in the midst of the Moabite community.

Prayer (v. 9): The third sentence of Naomi's first speech sets out the specifics of the kindness that Naomi prays God will manifest to the two younger women, namely, that each will find security through finding a new husband. Naomi's exhortation that they return to their mothers' houses assumes that the only or at least the best possibility for new husbands must be through their families in Moab. She holds to a traditional view that will persist in her repetition of the term "security" in the beginning of chapter 3, namely, that security for a woman comes from being married. Her hope is that the mother's house will soon be supplanted by the husband's house. Although the story of Ruth is one of women making decisions and taking action on their own, their action takes place in the context of this traditional assumption about women's place in socio-economic structure. Indeed, in Israel's society, such an assumption was probably realistic and prudent, as there appears to have been minimal structural provision for the well-being of unmarried adult women in that culture. The story appears to presume the same perspective within Moabite culture.

Nonetheless, it must be said that we know little of the customs for arranging marriages, much less second marriages, in either culture. Compounding our lack of information is the unusual fact of an inter-ethnic first marriage for these daughters-in-law. In addition, we are not sure about their ages, and we cannot be certain how long their childless marriages had endured (perhaps ten years, see v. 4). In the face of so many uncertainties, it is impossible to say whether their chances for remarriage in Moab were probable, possible, or essentially non-existent. Any interpretation of the motives of Orpah and Ruth in their respective decisions must take these unknowns into account.

The first cycle of this extended conversation ends with Naomi's 25 farewell kiss, weeping, and Ruth and Orpah's rejection of Naomi's proposal. The text does not make specific whether all three women wept or whether only the two daughters-in-law were weeping. The ambiguity is important because it and other similar uncertainties have led to the suggestion that Naomi is really desiring to return home to Judah alone. According to this interpretation, Naomi is not sending Ruth and Orpah to their mothers' households primarily out of kindness or concern for their future, but more out of self-interest, hoping not to be burdened with any further reminder of her family's failed expedition to Moab (Fewell and Gunn, pp. 28, 74). In this view, Naomi's words, while not technically untrue, do not reveal her true motives. Certainly the Bible, like literature generally, includes examples of speech designed to produce results from its insincere content. Fewell and Gunn's interpretation, however, seems strained as it reads nearly every speech in the entire story as disguising the speakers' true motives. Nonetheless, it is not unrealistic to imagine a greater degree of ambiguity of motivation in all the characters of this story than has usually been done.

The two daughters-in-law, rejecting Naomi's instruction, speak of "returning" with her to her people, even though of course they have never been to Judah. Here the verb indicates not so much a change of physical location as a change of social orientation. By repeated use of this verb (translated "turn," "return," "go back," or "turn back," according to context), Ruth and Orpah are pictured as turning from their Moabite roots to a Judahite familial and ethnic context, or vice versa. Physical departure is a way to continue and complete the turning that has already begun with their marriages. Certainly the storyteller is playing on this verb and wants readers to consider its various nuances, as the word occurs ten times in the three-part departure scene and twice more in the immediately-following arrival scene. The exact location of these occurrences is difficult to discern in English translations because other verbs are also translated "go back." Nonetheless, the English as a whole carries forward the flavor of the author's use of this verb to convey the ambiguity of where "home" lies for these women.

Second Speech and Response Cycle (1:11–14)

Naomi counters the insistence of her daughters-in-law by reiterating her exhortation and elaborating upon her arguments. She picks up Ruth and Orpah's unusual use of the verb "return" and places it in its more expected context—they are to "turn" (the same Hebrew verb), "go" (the same word Naomi used initially in v. 8). The NRSV here combines the two verbs into the single phrase "go back," although the narrator's use of the same verbs in reverse order in verse 7 is translated "they went on their way to go back." The storyteller's complex interweaving of the two verbs with both destinations and with all three characters serves to heighten the reader's sense of the complexity of relationships and loyalties in this inter-family, inter-ethnic, inter-geographical context, complexities that may be replicated in any era when families become entwined across such dividing lines.

Naomi continues with a powerful rhetorical reminder that she is in no position to provide the husbands she believes essential for the well-being of her daughters-in-law. She appears to describe herself as beyond the age of child-bearing; she views herself as too old to be marriageable. She emphasizes her point by imagining that some man might nonetheless look upon her to marry her and that she might nonetheless conceive—even in such a case it would be years before boy babies would be ready for marriage, and the daughters-in-law would not or should not wait. The reader is not told the ages of any of the story's characters, but if we begin with the common assumption that marriages in that culture usually took place during the mid-teen years, Naomi's perspective makes narrative sense. If she herself married at the age of fifteen, she would have been about thirty-two by the time her sons were fifteen and ready to enter into their marriages with Ruth and Orpah. If some or all of the ten years' time mentioned in verse 4 elapsed during the time of those marriages, Naomi could be as old as her early forties, with Ruth and Orpah in their mid-twenties. In a world where life expectancy was forty years or less, Naomi's insistence that she is not marriageable and that her daughters-in-law cannot wait another fifteen years or so for re-marriage is common sense, powerfully stated.

Yet one must ask why Naomi bothers with such rhetoric. Would anyone actually have supposed that she had some responsibility for providing blood descendants as new husbands for Ruth and Orpah? Scholars have long debated the relevance of the practice of levirate marriage (marriage of a widow to her husband's brother) to the story of Ruth as a whole and to these words of Naomi in particular. This practice of levirate marriage appears in the Old Testament in two texts: in a legal prescription in Deuteronomy 25:5–10 and in the story of Tamar in Genesis 38. The possibility of the theme of levirate marriage in the story of Ruth is raised in the first instance by Naomi's point that there are no prospects for brothers of Mahlon and Chilion for Ruth and Orpah to marry. It is compounded by the arrangement for Ruth to marry a "kinsman" in the concluding section of the story. The fact that a ceremony involving a sandal takes place at the city gate in Ruth 4 and an allusion to such a ceremony appears in Deuteronomy 25:9 heightens interest in this theme, as does the fact that the Tamar of Genesis 38 is remembered in Ruth 4:12 as the father of Perez, an ancestor of Boaz (vv. 18–22).

27

Yet there are many discrepancies between the details of Ruth 4 and the other biblical examples. These discrepancies make it questionable that levirate marriage is central to the transaction at the town gate (cf. Introduction, and commentary on 3:9b; 4:3–10). Nor is the general understanding of levirate marriage practice readily applicable to Naomi's words here in chapter 1. Her first statement (v. 11) is conceivably relevant if taken literally rather than as an allusion to menopause: she is not now carrying sons who might have been offspring of Elimelech. Only such sons could be full brothers to Mahlon and Chilion as envisaged in the scenarios of Deuteronomy 25 and Genesis 38. Yet even such a connection to levirate marriage would seem at best to be a rhetorical point, since the prologue (vv. 1–5) suggests that Elimelech may have been dead for many years. Naomi's speech does have in common with the Tamar story the theme of waiting for a son to become of age. But sons of Naomi by another husband (as imagined in her development of the theme of her childlessness, v. 12) could not fulfill the purpose of continuing the male line of descent unless the man were a brother of Elimelech, and Naomi expresses no such concern about the imagined husband. Her focus continues to be on the security of her daughters-in-law, on their protection and welfare, not on a blood tie for the "building up of the brother's house" (Deuteronomy 25:9).

Naomi's words should thus be taken not as a reference to levirate marriage, but as a heightened rhetorical expression of pain and frustration about her inability to provide care for her daughters-in-law, reinforcing the theme already expressed symbolically and religiously in her previous speech when she commended Ruth and Orpah to God's kindly care. By the end of the story Naomi's pain will be resolved, but not necessarily within the confines of levirate marriage.

Naomi climaxes her speech by bringing her frustration to stark expression in the end of verse 13. She speaks of her "bitterness" because God's hand is against her, a theme that is resumed in 1:20. Her words have progressed from strong advice to her daughters-in-law to strong statements of the impossibility of her provision for them to this strong statement of her own feeling in the face of the loss of her men-folk. The sequence is a very human one, as the logic of her own words spills over into a cry of pain over the situation itself. This focus on her own misery continues until changed circumstances lead her to look outward again in 2:20.

Three aspects of Naomi's words in verse 13b deserve note. First, the term *bitterness* can have various nuances. Although specific reasons for Naomi's bitterness are developed further in the next scene, verses 20–21, the particular range of this inner emotion is not further devel-

28

oped. Not only frustration, but despair, sadness, and even anger may be components of her bitterness.

Second, Naomi compares herself to her daughters-in-law. Although there is some debate about translation of the phrase, the comparative (as in NRSV) seems clearly preferable (Campbell, pp. 70–71). Although Naomi does not say why her situation is worse than theirs, the likely reasoning is apparent from her previous concern that they should be married again. They at least are of an age and social condition that Naomi imagines their remarriage to be possible. At her age, the possibility of renewed "security" by relationship to a husband appears nonexistent. At the same time, the death of her sons means that care for her old age, normally the responsibility of a couple's male children, is also absent from Naomi's horizon. The older, childless widow would appropriately regard herself as in desperate straits.

Finally, Naomi's outcry blames God for what has transpired in her life. This is the third reference to the LORD in the story. First, Naomi heard that the LORD had provided food (v. 6); then she asked that the LORD bless Ruth and Orpah (vv. 8–9); now she says that the LORD's hand has gone out against her. God can provide for peoples and for individual persons; but in Naomi's view God has not cared for her. While ancient Jewish and modern commentators speculate about the deaths of the men for disobedience in going to Moab or marrying Moabites, the story that we receive gives no attention to God's relationship to Elimelech, Mahlon and Chilion. Nor does the narrator claim that God had turned against Naomi. That is her perception, expressed in her speech. Unlike Job, she is not portrayed as being interested in why calamity has struck. Unlike those psalmists who uttered prayers of lament, she is not portrayed as asking God for a change in her condition; indeed, given the nature of her problem, a prayer for redress would not have been readily imaginable. Her spirit has been crushed even beyond the point of prayer. Yet as events unfold by the end of the story, the prayer not uttered because it could not even be imagined will nonetheless receive its answer.

The second cycle concludes with another time of weeping, followed by Orpah's departure. Although the narrator contrasts Orpah's separation kiss with Ruth's clinging to Naomi, it would be wrong to draw from this contrast a negative judgment on Orpah's behavior. The narrative itself offers no explicit evaluation of Orpah's decision. As explained above, little is known about the customs of the time, so we cannot know whether Naomi's advice was conventional or not, or what ancient hearers of the story would have expected Ruth and Orpah to do. The circumstances here may be so unusual that there were no

29

established norms for the choices to be made by these three women at the roadside.

Naturally the plot hinges upon Ruth's going with Naomi. Yet it must not be forgotten that Orpah was the one who followed Naomi's instructions. Assuming that Naomi meant her advice seriously as wise counsel for the younger women, she would surely have been pleased with Orpah's decision. To the extent that Naomi may have been ambivalent about the presence of her daughters-in-law on the journey, she may have been glad for her own sake as well as for Orpah's that her advice was accepted. If Ruth's choice was extraordinary, it does not make Orpah's more ordinary choice culpable; if Ruth's choice was less than extraordinary, then all the more must Orpah be freed from the blame wrongly placed upon her by the interpretive tradition. In many circumstances of life, two persons facing a common dilemma make different choices; rarely can outsiders know enough of the individual situations to know for sure which choices are heroic or sacrificial, which are appropriate and sensible, and which are morally questionable.

Ruth "clings" to Naomi. Although the verb "to cling" is not uncommon in Hebrew, the context here calls quickly to mind its use in the Genesis 2 account of the creation of the first man and woman. After the man's joyous exclamation over the discovery of one who is "bone of my bones," the narrator explains that "therefore a man leaves his father and his mother and clings to his wife . . ." (Gen. 2:24). The emotion that draws Ruth to Naomi may not be sexual (although some have made such a claim), but the power of the feeling that leads Ruth to leave behind her birth family in favor of a new loyalty must not be missed. The stage is set for the third section of this departure scene.

Third Speech and Response Cycle (1:15–18)

A third time Naomi speaks, now exhorting Ruth to follow Orpah's example. In this final effort Naomi introduces a new element. The issue of family and marriage has disappeared. Perhaps she saw that it was having no impact on Ruth; perhaps she recalled something else about Ruth's background. In any case, she mentions not just Orpah's people, but her gods. It is the Moabites and Moabite religion that are now in view. Naomi urges Ruth to stick with her own people and religious tradition.

Ruth's response has become well known because of its popularity in many Christian marriage ceremonies, sometimes as a commitment of bride to new husband, sometimes as words of mutual commitment. Few who use it in that context are aware of the original setting of these lines as the commitment of one woman to another, one widow to another, a daughter-in-law to her mother-in-law. Equally missing is the sense that one of the parties is resisting the express desire of the other as these words are spoken. Thus the opening line, "do not press me to leave you," would be inappropriate in wedding ceremonies and is rarely cited.

In this opening line, the verb "to leave" may have the general connotation of "to depart from," but it often carries the stronger sense of "to abandon." As in 1:14, the verb used echoes Genesis 2:24 and reinforces the reader's sense of the personal bond Ruth feels toward Naomi. Ruth further expresses her rejection of Naomi's instruction with yet another use of the verb "to turn back" (see comment above), in direct response to Naomi's double use of that same terminology for what Orpah has done.

Ruth's promise to Naomi moves through several stages of intensity. The commitment to go with Naomi and to lodge with her incorporates the personal dimension of the companionship and support Ruth offers to her mother-in-law. To commit herself in this way to Naomi is no small thing, regardless of her prospects in Moab. If she might easily have been remarried in Moab, then she has chosen an old woman over a young man (Trible, p. 173). Even if her prospects in Moab were not good in her own thinking, commitment to stick with an older woman whose reception at home is uncertain is still a striking decision. In today's cultures, even in those where the elderly are honored and where care for them by family members is assumed, the younger generation is well aware of the financial difficulties and personal demands that may be incurred as a parent ages. Whatever Ruth's motives, she was presumably wise enough to know of potential difficulties in the path she was setting for herself.

To journey and to live together can take place within a limited, albeit still significant, level of commitment. Ruth's next promises, that Naomi's people and Naomi's God will be hers as well, mark major additional steps. Her words repeat verbatim and thus stand in explicit rejection of Naomi's last plea that Ruth follow the example of Orpah, who had returned to her own people and gods. Commitment to another people across ethnic and cultural lines need not mean abandoning one's own identity (people today often speak of their "dual identity"), but such commitment does require intentional effort. It may mean commitment to learn about the other's culture, to gain acquaintance with its language or dialect, to cook its traditional foods or to learn its folklore. The task is usually not so easy as it appears from the outside; there may or may not be encouragement from the insiders, and the difficulty of fully grasping and appropriating a different culture often becomes more and more apparent as years pass by.

31

For Ruth the commitment to accept Naomi's people as her own is made in the face of possible, even probable, rejection by that people. As Ruth expresses her intent, readers must imagine that she is aware that the people of Judah are unlikely to accept a Moabite as a member of their community. This reality is in fact highlighted further in the story by the repeated references to her as "the Moabite." Her ethnic identity stands as a barrier that must be challenged to enable her full inclusion in the new community. Ruth is risking much in committing herself to Naomi's people.

In reflecting upon Ruth's commitment to a new people and a new geographic location, Asian-American theologians have highlighted the danger of using Ruth's decision as a warrant for an assimilationist, melting-pot view of the proper role of immigrants to the United States (Sano, p. 299). In fact, the story of Ruth does not claim that she totally assimilates or abandons her cultural identity. The repeated references to her Moabite ancestry point not only to resistance in Bethlehem, but also to her legitimate claim to participate as a Moabite in the life of the Bethlehem community. Ethnic particularity is not denigrated by the story as a whole. At the same time, Ruth's migration and her claim to Naomi's geographic home offer the encouragement of pilgrimage imagery to immigrants of our own time as they strive to do God's will in their adoptive land (Lee, pp. 328–30).

Ruth's formal commitment to a different religious faith is a still more momentous decision, for in the case of religion (unlike general ethnic or cultural identity) an abandoning of the former faith is expected. In Jewish tradition, Ruth is remembered as the paradigmatic example of conversion. Rabbinic writers interpreted her speech as a declaration of conversion and deduced from her words requirements to be accepted by all converts. A "catechism of proselytism" was developed in which each of her phrases was related to aspects of Jewish life, ranging from rejecting idolatry to limiting travel on the Sabbath, to regulations about forms of capital punishment, to the requirement for a mezuzah on the doorpost of a Jewish home (Beattie, pp. 173–75).

For many who read this story as lifelong Jews or lifelong Christians, the magnitude of a decision such as Ruth's may be hard to appreciate. So long as it seems self-evident that one's own faith is the right and even the only way to believe and worship, it can be difficult to grasp why others do not respond in the same way, or to consider the cost to them in acknowledging a different God or a different way of conceiving of God. On the other hand, many modern persons who tend to think of all religions as "basically alike," or who have migrated easily from one faith tradition to another to yet another, or who do not feel an abiding attachment to any one religious tradition, will also have difficulty in appreciating Ruth's decision. Although the storyteller does not provide details, the contrast between Naomi's advice and Ruth's response suggests a deliberate choice for a different deity and way of life. The name of the traditional Moabite deity Chemosh is known from biblical and extrabiblical sources, but not much is known of that religion. Whatever the character of Chemosh worship, however, the perspective of the Israelite storyteller is that the LORD (Yahweh) alone is God; Ruth's commitment is not to worship Yahweh as an addition to some polytheistic pantheon of her own, but rather to entrust herself completely to this God of whom she has presumably learned from Naomi and her dead husband.

Finally, Ruth states her intention to make a life-long commitment. She will die where Naomi dies and be buried with her. There is more at stake here than the length of time of the commitment. In cultures of the ancient Near East, burial in one's ancestral homeland was considered extremely important. The biblical narrative of the transporting of Joseph's bones back from Egypt to land purchased by his father Jacob (Joshua 24:32; cf. Gen. 50:24–26) illustrates this tradition. By insisting that she will be buried with Naomi, Ruth is further distancing herself from her homeland. In a sense this third promise is a capstone for the personal commitment and for the commitment to Naomi's people and God. The commitment is now pictured as complete and irrevocable.

Ruth's promise concludes with an oath before the LORD (Naomi's God) that reconfirms this last step. The pledge that she will not allow even death to part her from Naomi should not be taken as a reference to resurrection or to life after death, which was not a part of the Hebrew thought world until very late. Rather the oath reconfirms the permanence and strength of Ruth's commitment. She does not intend to stand by Naomi only until Naomi dies, and then to return to Moab. Rather, she will remain committed to Naomi's people and God and be buried with Naomi. Furthermore, if her new commitment should bring any threat to Ruth's own life, even then she will not abandon her commitment to Naomi, her people, and her God. In view of this strength of commitment, the ancient rabbis as well as more recent commentators have set Ruth alongside Abraham, who also left his family and homeland. Indeed, Ruth's action is even more memorable than Abraham's, for she acts without a specific revelation from God, without any divine word of calling or blessing (Trible, p. 173; Darr, p. 72).

While Ruth's commitment is generally praised for its radical and even sacrificial nature, two caveats introduced earlier must be reiterated. First, we do not know anything of the circumstances that led Ruth

33

to this commitment. Certainly she made a radical choice; but it is possible that Naomi's contrary advice made no sense for Ruth's situation. Perhaps her family had already rejected her because of her marriage to an outsider. Perhaps her family was in such dire econmic straits that feeding another mouth would have been impossible to contemplate. Perhaps she had reason to know that there would be no marriage prospects for her in Moab. As we praise Ruth for choosing in favor of the unknown, we need to realize that only interpreters, not the text itself, have created the "known" that Ruth is abandoning.

Second, we must be cautious about generalizing Ruth's words to her mother-in-law as a desirable model for all women. Modern cultures vary in their views of the relationships between mothers-in-law and daughters-in-law. In western contexts, the relationship is the occasion for jokes based on criticism or ill-will, and discussions about strained relationships with in-laws are mixed with stories of good will. Yet there are no culturally consistent patterns of expectations for the mother-in-law/daughter-in-law relationship. In some other parts of the world, by contrast, this relationship is culturally highly prescribed. The daughter-in-law is in some cases expected to become the virtual servant of her husband's parents, and especially of his mother. In such settings, stories of various forms of oppression and restriction of the daughter-in-law are legion. In some Christian circles, both Western and in other parts of the globe, Ruth's commitment to Naomi is used to exhort all young women to sacrifice everything for their mothers-in-law. Against this use of the story, the larger context should be remembered. Ruth makes a choice; Naomi does not expect it, indeed discourages it; and the choice is made not in the normal course of events of married life, but in the context of unmitigated family disaster that calls for unusual decisions. In sum, the loyalty of Ruth to Naomi may offer a general model for loyal relationships between all people, not just for daughter-in-law to mother-in-law. At the same time, the story of Ruth models loyalty freely offered to another, not coerced by custom, culture, or biblical demand.

The third speech and response cycle (and the scene by the roadside as a whole) closes with Naomi's realization that Ruth's mind cannot be changed. With that realization, Naomi "said no more to her." This concluding word from the narrator rounds off the three-fold cycle of speeches and responses. While the first two cycles ended with weeping and physical contact, the third ends with no action, only silence. There is no direct indication whether Naomi is inwardly pleased or displeased with Ruth's decision, but the texture of the larger narrative presses toward displeasure or, at the very best, ambivalence. Ruth has not accepted the advice of a wiser, older woman, the advice of a woman who may in that culture have held authority over her. In the next scene, the arrival in Bethlehem, Naomi makes no acknowledgment of Ruth. She subsequently gives Ruth permission to go gleaning (2:2), but with a terseness that is noticeable in a book filled with many longer speech quotations. The reader's honoring and appreciating of Ruth's choice must be tempered by the thought that Ruth is offering an undesired "gift," even though in this case all turns out well in the end. Naomi's silence may be interpreted as despair, anger, or resignation—in her own word, bitterness. For Naomi, Ruth's presence is as much a reminder of tragedy as it is a potential comfort. Naomi has no idea how she herself will be received upon returning to Bethlehem, and now she has also a foreign companion to be explained. She may have realized that if Ruth had stayed in Moab, perhaps no one in Judah would have learned of her sons' marriages. Is Ruth to be primarily a reminder of the past or will she become a source of hope for the future? The stage is set for the next phase of the story.

Ruth 1:19–22
Arrival in Bethlehem

This brief unit rounds out the opening chapter by bringing the scene back to Bethlehem and encapsulating the result of what has transpired in the previous paragraphs. The journey to Bethlehem is reported in one brief sentence, half a verse, only six words in Hebrew. Although we do not know how far along on the journey the three women had been before Naomi's triple exhortation and Orpah's departure, the brevity of this report signals that nothing of significance transpires as Naomi and Ruth walk together. We are left to imagine that Naomi's silence continues. At their arrival in Bethlehem, the whole town is filled with excitement. Travelers from afar may or may not have been frequent, but two women arriving alone would certainly cause comment. Apparently it is the women of the town who first recognize the older arrival, although even they are not certain. "Is this Naomi?" they ask. The ten or more intervening years of toil and tragedy, let alone the hardships of the journey, have taken their toll on Naomi's appearance, and the expected clues for confirmation of identity that anyone looks to on sighting a long-lost friend are missing—no husband, no sons, only an accompanying woman stranger.

To their recognizing query, Naomi offers a response that summarizes with some irony the tragedy that has befallen her. "Call me no

35

longer Naomi [i.e., sweetness, pleasantness], call me Mara [bitterness]."
As in her words to her daughters-in-law (v. 13), she again points to God
as the author of her tragedy, twice using the name Yahweh (the LORD),
twice speaking of God as Shaddai, an ancient name for God traditionally translated as "the Almighty." This God, the only one she knows, has
"dealt bitterly," "dealt harshly," "brought calamity." Like Job, she can
see no reason and sees no way out. Like Jeremiah in his laments (e.g.,
Jer. 15:15–18; 20:7–10), she describes graphically the extent of her pain
and lays its source squarely in the only place possible from her point of
view. Unlike Job and Jeremiah, however, Naomi does not ask why, does
not ask for redress. She is physically alive, but from an emotional and
psychological point of view, she views her life as already over.

Naomi speaks of leaving Bethlehem "full" but being brought back
(returned) by God "empty." The family left with empty bellies but
complete as a family. What matter is food to Naomi if there is no family? Now she is "empty," bereft of what really made her life worth living. The presence of Ruth goes completely unremarked as she explains
the absence of her husband and sons as God's calamity. Ironically also,
Naomi states that it is God who has brought her back. In verse 6, the
decision to return was described as Naomi's. Here as she speaks of her
return as God's action, action in which she now sees nothing but sorrow, Naomi unknowingly anticipates the ways in which God will continue to work behind the scenes for the redemption of her tragedy.

In considering Naomi's bitterness, one must come to terms with
more than the socio-economic marginalization of a childless widow in
Israelite culture. The reality of the loss of a beloved spouse or of a child,
or children, let alone all of one's immediate blood family, is devastating
emotionally to most people in most cultures. The fact that death was a
more frequent and earlier visitor to Israelite families than to many in
the modern world does not make Naomi's losses any less painful or easier to bear. Readers of this story who have grieved deeply themselves
or who have accompanied a close friend or relative on that path will
more easily grasp the way in which this entire book may be read as a
story about Naomi as much as one about Ruth. Certainly Naomi is the
central figure in the opening chapter. It is her loss and her despair that
must be addressed in what follows.

The narrator concludes the report of the women's return with a
reprise of the event (v. 22), reintroducing Ruth, whom Naomi had ignored, and reminding the reader of Ruth's double identity as Moabite
and daughter-in-law. God's gift of food, the theme of full or empty, and
the context for the following chapter are all lifted up implicitly in the
notice that it was "the beginning of the barley harvest."

36

PART TWO

Feeding a Family

RUTH 2

Naomi has returned home because she heard "that the LORD had considered his people and given them food" (1:6). But the presence of food in general does not necessarily supply sustenance for any particular family. So it is that Ruth proposes to go out to glean. In the context of Ruth's gleaning, chapter 2 presents the meeting of Ruth and Boaz and climaxes with Naomi's reaction to that event. Although it is a unified whole, the chapter is made up of three main scenes with several sub-parts. The first scene involves Ruth and Naomi; this is followed by a scene involving Ruth and Boaz and a final scene again featuring Ruth and Naomi. After a word of background information from the narrator (v. 1), a brief conversation between Naomi and Ruth leads to Ruth's arrival in the field (vv. 2–3). Boaz learns from his head reaper who the unknown woman is (vv. 4–7). Then Boaz and Ruth have an extended conversation (vv. 8–13); subsequently they share a midday meal and he makes special provision for a more generous food-gathering opportunity for her (vv. 14–17). Finally, as Ruth returns home in the evening she and Naomi converse about her day's activity (vv. 18–23).

Ruth 2:1–3
Ruth and Naomi

Introducing Boaz (2:1)

As the chapter opens, the narrator provides essential information about Boaz so that the reader can take anticipatory delight in the events soon to transpire. The reader needs to know who Boaz is in relation to Naomi and to Bethlehem in order to assess each aspect of the various conversations that follow in the rest of the chapter. Unlike the introduction of Elimelech in 1:2, this introduction begins not with "a certain man" but rather with Naomi. Of prime importance concerning Boaz is that he is related to her on her husband's side, from the clan (NRSV "family") of Elimelech. The scope of extended family included in the Hebrew "clan" may be quite broad. It should be noted that the Hebrew term used here for her husband's "kinsman" (NRSV) is not the more familiar Hebrew word for a "next-of-kin"/"redeemer" (gōʾēl), which often connotes specific legal responsibilities for protection of family members. This word gōʾēl will appear, but only later in the story. The word used in 2:1 may be a synonym for gōʾēl (so Campbell, pp. 88–89); or it may indicate some overlapping circle of relationship with different connotations. In either case, the curiosity of the hearer is still aroused: will Boaz's relationship to Naomi make any real difference to the course of events?

The narrator further describes Boaz as a "prominent rich man" (gibbôr ḥayil, literally a "mighty man of power, a worthy man"), indicating his high standing in the Bethlehem community. In this case, the phrase also connotes material wealth, as is confirmed a few verses later when his status as owner of a field and employer of hired workers is revealed. The narrator's use of gibbôr ḥayil is significant in two respects. First, it places Boaz at great social distance from the poverty-stricken returnee Naomi and her foreign daughter-in-law. This contrast is heightened by the placement of the phrase: the description of Boaz as a prominent citizen is flanked on either side with phrases that point to his kinship relationship to Naomi. Second, Boaz will subsequently speak of Ruth as an ʾēšet ḥayil, a woman of worth (3:11), thus collapsing literarily the socio-cultural distance between them.

The information in verse 1 is essential to the reader and is generally taken as an aside by the narrator to the audience (so NRSV). Sasson, however, has translated the verse to mean that Naomi is already thinking about Boaz: "Now Naomi knew an acquaintance of her husband . . . " (pp. 38–39). It is certainly true that Naomi later recognizes Boaz's name and knows of his relationship to her (2:20), but Sasson's translation is problematic on two grounds. First, it is difficult syntactically. Furthermore, if Naomi has Boaz consciously in mind before Ruth goes out gleaning, the reader must wonder why Naomi does nothing with the information that is on her mind, even when Ruth speaks of her hope to find someone to look favorably on her. Ruth goes out uninformed. On balance, the usual view of the verse as a narrator's aside makes greater syntactic and narrative sense.

Ruth and Naomi (2:2–3)

The narrator again uses the phrase "Ruth the Moabite" that was introduced in 1:22 as soon as she arrived in Bethlehem. The phrase will appear repeatedly; from beginning to end the reader must not be allowed to forget her foreign status. Ruth speaks to Naomi of going out to glean, hoping for a kindly reception from someone in the field of the village farmers. The NRSV "let me go out" is ambiguous in English; the Hebrew construction suggests more a statement of intention than a request for permission, although Naomi's reply suggests that she gives consent. Naomi's response is as brief as possible; she seems still caught up in her grief and bitterness, unable to take any step or assist with any plan for her own survival. She does address Ruth as "my daughter," perhaps an indication that she has not entirely rejected their relationship; on the other hand, this might be simply courteous address to a younger woman, as Boaz uses the same expression in verse 8. Ruth, by contrast to Naomi, dares to take initiative to support the two of them, even though her words show that she anticipates possible resistance to her presence.

Gleaning is a primary means of support for the destitute prescribed in Israelite law. The basic prescriptions are found in Leviticus 19:9–10, 23:22 and Deuteronomy 24:19–22. The edges of fields are not to be harvested, and the "gleanings," that is, what is not picked up in the first pass-through of those who bundle the grain-stalks, also shall be left behind for the alien, the poor, the orphan and the widow. As a poor non-Israelite widow, Ruth seeks out this means of survival designated for her by Israelite law. Gleaning continues in various forms in the modern world as a means of survival for the destitute. In some countries, it is structured by law, routinized as a welfare safety net, or organized through food banks; but even there, people rummage through garbage cans to survive. In some poorer nations, conditions for the destitute in search of food are even more extreme.

As the narrator reports Ruth's arrival in the field (v. 3), we have a picture of a communal village field, with certain parts nonetheless designated as belonging to various individuals. Ruth is already at work reaping as the narrator informs the audience that "as it happened," she began working in the portion belonging to "Boaz, who was of the

39

family of Elimelech." Boaz's relationship to Elimelech's family is repeated, even though it was given only two verses earlier. This pattern of reiteration of key information follows that already identified in 1:1, 2 and 1:6, 7. At this stage, the narrator allows us to imagine that Ruth arrived in Boaz's portion of the field by chance; the Jewish Publication Society even translates, "by chance," and so it might seem. But in this story God is at work behind the scenes; what appears as chance is better to be understood as divine providence (cf. comment at 2:20; Hals, pp. 11–13). Although none of the characters is yet aware, and although there are many hurdles yet to be overcome, a corner has been turned, a crack in a seemingly impenetrable wall has appeared, the beginning of a possible path from death to life, from bitterness to joy has been shown to the readers. It remains to be seen whether the characters will act in ways that enable God's intention for wholeness to be realized.

Ruth 2:4–17
Boaz and Ruth

Boaz Inquires about Ruth (2:4–7)

It so happened that Ruth came to the portion of the field belonging to Boaz. Now in further apparent coincidence, Boaz just happens to come out to the field to check on the progress of the work. He addresses his workers with words of blessing that were probably the common parlance of greeting, and they reply in kind. In most of modern Western Christianity such words of mutual blessing are best known from their liturgical use as the preface to times of prayer: "the Lord be with you. . . . and also with you." The older custom of such greetings in everyday settings has disappeared with increasing secularization of society. Likewise, the Christian custom of beginning written correspondence to other Christians with greetings in the manner of St. Paul, "grace to you . . . " or "greetings in the name of our Lord," has largely disappeared in the West, although happily it is retained in other parts of Christendom. Frequent use of such greetings may have made them perfunctory in ancient Israel, even as our English "goodbye" no longer conveys its original meaning of "God be with you." In this instance, however, the greeting is incorporated into a narrative that is shot through with occasions in which characters invoke divine blessing upon one another (1:8; 2:12; 2:19, 20; 3:10; 4:11). In such a setting, Boaz's greeting should be read with its full theological meaning. The third principal character, Boaz appears on stage giving and receiving divine blessing.

Immediately Boaz inquires about a gleaner whom he does not recognize. In a small town or village, an unknown person was quickly noticeable. He does not speak to Ruth directly; he does not ask her name, he does not ask where she came from. He asks to whom she belongs. The meaning and tone are not so crass as the English translation might suggest, although the question is certainly an indication that women were not thought of as or expected to be independent persons. Boaz is asking after her family connection, wondering whose wife, daughter, or servant she might be; the name of that person is more important than her own. The same expression is used elsewhere concerning male household servants (Gen. 32:18; I Sam. 30:13). The response from the man in charge of the reapers supplies Boaz with a possible family connection, but Ruth does not fit the paradigm that requires a man's name in response to Boaz's question. Nor does the head reaper's reply explain her familial relationship to Naomi. Since the subsequent conversation between Boaz and Ruth reveals that he already knows her story (v. 11), perhaps Boaz knows what her name and the relationship must be once he is told that she had accompanied Naomi. Literarily, the absence of Ruth's name, coupled with the double reference to her ethnic background as a Moabite who came from Moab, serves to highlight the villagers' view of Ruth. She is "that foreigner." Although it is said that she accompanied Naomi, even her place as daughter-in-law is likewise omitted in favor of emphasis on her outsider status.

The head reaper has more to say, but the Hebrew text of verse 7 is difficult; in fact, the preserved Hebrew text of the last half of the verse makes no sense. The textual problem is very old, as can be seen from the efforts of the early Greek and Latin translators to create sense out of the head reaper's concluding statement. Every modern proposal for translating requires significant textual emendations; generally these proposals serve the translators' pre-understandings of what must be happening in the story at this point. Campbell is probably right that the problems are too numerous to allow full confidence in any solution (pp. 94–96). Furthermore, even the first part of verse 7 is awkward because what Ruth requests is the same as what Boaz specially arranges in verse 15. (The NRSV obscures this problem by distinguishing between "sheaves" [v. 7] and "standing sheaves" [v. 15], although the Hebrew expression is the same.) With regard to this latter problem, some propose simply to omit "among the sheaves" in verse 7a, so that Ruth begins her gleaning only where all the reapers' work had been completed, that is, where the sheaves have already been removed. Ancient translations provide precedent for this approach.

Whether this solution helps the story line depends upon how the more difficult final part of the verse is handled. Three main scenarios are possible: (1) As suggested in the NRSV translation, Ruth's petition was granted immediately by the head reaper. She has been working continuously and is working as Boaz arrives. (2) Ruth has worked for a long period but is taking a rest break as Boaz arrives. Nielsen adopts this view and suggests that Boaz noticed Ruth because she was resting rather than because she was an unknown figure among the other working gleaners (p. 58). (3) The head reaper has no authority to give Ruth an answer to her petition, so she has simply been standing by, awaiting the arrival of the owner Boaz. This is the very tentative suggestion of Campbell (p. 96). Its plausibility depends upon taking verse 3a as a proleptic summary of what will transpire. This interpretation of 3a is unusual but not impossible, especially given the examples of introductory statements followed by resumption of the story line adduced above in interpreting 1:2b and 1:7.

From either of the first two scenarios, it is possible to describe Ruth as diligent and hardworking. Anyone who has done bend-over field labor knows how much rest breaks are needed and how tempting it is to extend them just a little. The head reaper praises her or at least admires her for her efforts, despite his emphasis on her status as foreigner. Within the third scenario, we may imagine Ruth as a person of determination and patience, although it is not clear why she would not have gone to another field rather than awaiting the possible but not certain arrival of Boaz. Her hours of waiting would be more plausible if she knew already who Boaz was; but as suggested above, the overall flow of the story, especially the narrator's highlighting of coincidence/divine providence, argues against Ruth's advance knowledge of Boaz's identity.

On balance, the first solution, implicit in the NRSV translation, seems most probable. Fortunately the decision about this difficult verse does not control the reader's understanding of the continuing progress of the story. Whether Ruth is gleaning, resting from gleaning, or still awaiting permission to glean at the moment Boaz first sees her, the initiative is now his, and he approaches her with instruction and advice.

42

Boaz Speaks with Ruth (2:8–17)

Boaz's initial words to Ruth (vv. 8–9) stick strictly to the subject of her work as a gleaner. Yet he goes far beyond simply granting or confirming permission for Ruth to work in his field. First of all, he invites, even urges her to work only in his field, not to go elsewhere. Second, he gives practical advice as to how she should behave. She should stick close to Boaz's young women and keep her eyes down. The verb translated "keep close" is the same verb that earlier expressed Ruth's "clinging" to Naomi (1:14; see comment there). There Ruth's closeness to Naomi expressed her affection and protective care for Naomi; now the same term is used as advice for Ruth's own protection. That these instructions are for Ruth's safety is confirmed by Boaz's command to the young men not to bother (Jewish Publication Society translates "molest") her. It is quite possible that any young woman working alone in the fields might be subject to unsolicited advances by men in the area. The risk of such advances would doubtless be greater in cases where it was known that the woman had no male protector. A foreigner from a disliked ethnic group would be even more likely to be victimized. Boaz concludes his words by inviting Ruth to share in the water supplied for his own workers. Although we do not know any details of the customs surrounding gleaning, it is quite likely that this was a special privilege not usually granted.

Thus Boaz advises Ruth how to see to her own well-being in such a situation. But before even speaking to her, he has taken a further step: by instructing his young men not to bother her, Boaz has in effect established himself in their eyes as Ruth's male protector. Whether Boaz would have done this for any such young woman, or whether he took this step because of his kinship to Naomi we do not know. Fewell and Gunn suggest that his action may also have been motivated by a nascent personal attraction to Ruth; his arrangements would seem to reduce the possibility of male competition (pp. 42, 84–85). There is no reason that only one of these motives must prevail at the expense of all others, although personal attraction receives no explicit mention anywhere in the story. Boaz is at once the upright citizen, the helpful relative, and the unmarried land owner. In the design of the story as a whole, however, the picture of Boaz as the relative who offers protection should be foregrounded. Here we have the storyteller's adumbration of the successful conclusion to the tale, the first note of confirmation that it was indeed divine providence that brought Ruth to this particular field.

Ruth's reply (v. 10) recognizes that what Boaz has offered is special privilege. She has achieved what she had hoped for (v. 2), permission to glean behind someone in whose sight she has found favor. Indeed, what has transpired exceeds her initial hope, which envisaged only a reaper who would show favor, presumably by not cleaning the field too thoroughly. Now the very owner of the field has shown favor to her and will

43

soon instruct his workers to leave extra grain for her (v. 16). She prostrates herself before Boaz, thanking him by what she probably intends as a rhetorical question as to his motivation in assisting a foreign woman.

If Ruth's question was meant rhetorically, she would have expected no substantive answer. If it was a serious question, she might well have expected Boaz to hint at some service, even sexual favors, that she should provide for him in exchange. In either case, his reply (vv. 11–12) must have come as a welcome surprise. Boaz has already heard, presumably through the Bethlehem grapevine, all about Ruth's situation, perhaps even more detail than the storyteller has felt necessary to provide us as readers. As Boaz speaks of what Ruth has done for Naomi, his words develop in a direction that focuses on her insistence on sticking by Naomi, in "leaving" (or abandoning, the same term found in 1:16) her own family (here father and mother) and land to place herself in the midst of a new people. Certainly Boaz's words suggest that he views Ruth's behavior as exceptional. In short, he reorients the assessment of her status as foreigner: she is deserving not of rejection or of grudging tolerance, but of honor and reward.

Although Boaz's words focus on Ruth's best known and most dramatic act on behalf of Naomi, it is possible that his words "all that you have done . . . since the death of your husband" look back also to Ruth's previous acts of kindness (*hesed,* see above at 1:8) to Naomi while in Moab. Naomi has earlier spoken of Ruth and Orpah's kindness (*hesed*) to her during the time in Moab (1:8), and Boaz will later (3:10) refer to Ruth's behavior in relation to Naomi with this same term. Although the noun *hesed* does not appear in 2:11, the substantive theme is present; and the verbal phrase "all you have done" is evocative of the standard Hebrew idiom "to do *hesed*" (NRSV "deal kindly with . . . dealt with . . . ") used in 1:8.

Boaz's positive view of Ruth's actions and presence is confirmed in his prayer on her behalf. His prayer is not just that she receive divine reward, but reward specifically from "the LORD, the God of Israel." His recounting of Ruth's deeds has already brought to the reader's mind her words of commitment to Naomi's person and to her people; now his prayer calls to mind her words of commitment to Naomi's God. It is that God, named by name and identified as the God of Naomi's people Israel, who is asked to recompense the loyal action of this erstwhile stranger. By her words of commitment, by her action in accompanying Naomi, by her presence among the people and the land belonging to the God of Israel, she has already sought shelter under Yahweh's wings. Now Boaz asks that that shelter yield concrete change in Ruth's life.

Although the powerful and beautiful imagery of God's protective wings as a place of refuge appears elsewhere only in Psalm 91:4, the motif of God as refuge appears in various contexts, for example, Deuteronomy 32:37 and Psalm 46. A reading of Psalm 91 may lead one to think first of disease or war, but it is possible to read the Psalm imagining that Ruth may have prayed it herself, or that Boaz's prayer on her behalf extended to incorporate this Psalm. The image of refuge, the language of care and protection, of deliverance and honor, and the theme of the overcoming of dire adversity all comport well with Ruth's story. We might even wish that Naomi in her pain were able to pray such a prayer. The psalm promises divine deliverance for those who trust in God as refuge, but it does not tell us how such rescue will come about. Naomi and Boaz now have both prayed that God will deal kindly with Ruth, will recompense her good work, but as yet we do not see how these prayers will be answered. The first hints of the answer will come in 2:14, and the theme of sheltering wings will be reprised in human context in 3:9 (NRSV "cloak") as part of the fuller answer.

In Ruth's response (v. 13) to Boaz's words (has she remained face down to the ground during his words of praise?), we again see the humble and deferential demeanor of a woman who has technical legal rights for gleaning but is still dependent upon the willingness of the owner or overseer to obey the law and allow her to work. For the third time, she speaks of finding favor; it seems that even Boaz's words have not fully reassured her. She appears almost timid, quite by contrast to her demeanor in her forthright disagreement with Naomi in chapter 1. She speaks of herself as Boaz's servant, a general term indicating lower rank, then hastens to correct or clarify her own statement—she does not really belong to his household, even in the servant class. Again the storyteller is inviting readers to enjoy their knowledge of Boaz's kinship relation to Naomi, information not yet known to Ruth. In fact Ruth is much more than servant to Boaz, but here she still speaks from her ignorance.

The text does not make the overall time-frame completely clear, but presumably some time elapses before the workers stop for a midday meal. Boaz again approaches Ruth. Probably imagining rightly that she has no food with her, he invites her to sit with his own workers and to share the food provided. It is not a private tryst but a gesture of inclusion into the larger community. Anticipating her reticence, he serves her more than she can possibly eat. Again his actions go beyond what is expected. Not only is Ruth fed; her status as a person to be accepted is demonstrated to the other workers. The story from start to finish illustrates the ways in which loyal action, kindness, and good will produce a

45

surplus that can both break down dividing walls of hostility and open new horizons to shattered lives.

As the meal concludes, Boaz instructs his workers to offer Ruth extra privileges beyond those ordinarily allowed to gleaners. First (following the NRSV), she may work among the standing sheaves, rather than restrict her work to areas where the field has already been cleared. In addition, the workers are actually to remove grain stalks from bundles that have already been made, leaving the stalks in her path! This new development makes most sense if one follows ancient versions that omit the reference to sheaves in verse 7 (see above). Boaz's insistence that his own workers not reproach or rebuke Ruth suggests, however, that she already may have been more aggressive in her gathering than was the general custom. It is difficult to reconcile this possibility with her extreme humility in speaking with Boaz, but both the generous meal and the expanded gleaning opportunity may be his response to her repeated request (v. 13) to receive his favor.

With this special privilege, Ruth's gleanings amount to about an ephah of unhusked grain by the end of the day. This amount (estimated at about 42 quarts) could feed two people for about five to seven days (Hamlin, p. 35). While gleaning provided an important safety net for the poorest of the poor in Israelite society, the results of Ruth's effort serve as a reminder that this safety net was flimsy at best and offered only a short-term solution to the problem of economic survival for persons like Ruth and Naomi. The days of gleaning will be as few as the days of harvesting, traditionally seven weeks for the entire village holdings; such an amount of grain could not fend off starvation for an extended period of time. Boaz's generosity is evident, but it is not sufficient to reverse Naomi and Ruth's economic hardship. They are better off than a day ago, but the future remains bleak unless a longer-term solution can be put in place.

Ruth 2:18–23
Ruth and Naomi

At home with Naomi, Ruth shows her mother-in-law first the harvested grain, then the parched grain left over from her meal with Boaz's reapers. Naomi, obviously impressed, asks where Ruth has worked, already invoking blessing upon the unknown "man who took notice of you" (v. 19). The storyteller holds off the mention of Boaz's name until the last moment, as readers realize that what may be of crucial importance is not

46

yet of significance to Ruth. Ruth's announcement that she had worked with Boaz evokes a response from Naomi that may be regarded as the turning point of the story both theologically and rhetorically. Naomi's spirit has already begun to quicken as she saw the generous results of Ruth's work. Now her words show signs that she imagines her life might begin again. In her excitement she offers a second blessing before she even explains to Ruth the reason for her reaction.

The Hebrew of Naomi's response in v. 20 is remarkably constructed. In invoking blessing on Boaz, Naomi speaks of one "whose kindness (*hesed*) has not forsaken [again the verb "to leave, abandon" appears, see 1:16 and 2:11] the living or the dead." In English rendering of the Hebrew, the natural referent for the relative pronoun "whose" is the nearest antecedent, "the LORD." But the Hebrew syntax is ambiguous, allowing the possibility that the pronoun "he," i.e., Boaz, may also be understood as an antecedent, as one whose kindness has not forsaken the living or the dead. In such a carefully crafted narrative, it seems possible that the ambiguity may be deliberate, that the storyteller invites us to explore and reflect upon this dual possibility. What might it mean in this setting to consider both Boaz and God as doers of acts of loyal kindness?

God has surely shown kindness, even as Naomi had asked in her words of blessing (1:8). In the providence of God, Ruth has come into the field that belonged to Boaz—Ruth's choice of location was indeed due to providence, not chance. Likewise it was by God's providence, not mere chance, that Boaz came to the field and saw Ruth there. Naomi may also attribute Boaz's generous and caring attitude toward Ruth to the kindness of God. After all, if special care for Ruth had been a simple result to achieve, and if Naomi had not been in such a bitter and despairing state, Naomi might have spoken to Boaz herself about such a possibility.

God's kindness is not limited to Ruth; Naomi's words encompass "the living," thus also herself, and "the dead," thus also her husband and sons. In Hebrew, the words "living" and "dead" are both masculine plural forms, so perhaps Naomi is speaking a formulaic word of blessing here, as was suggested also for 1:8. How what has happened so far relates to her dead family members is not made explicit and is less easy to discern. Perhaps the reference to kindness to the dead is to be understood proleptically. By God's kindness, recognized through Boaz's action, the door is now ajar and developments that will transpire by the end of the story begin to be imaginable. Elimelech's land will be redeemed, There will be a male child, described as "son to Naomi," (what she had deemed impossible in 1:11) who will be "a restorer of life and a nourisher of [her] old age" (4:15).

47

In what sense may it be said that Boaz too has acted loyally or with kindness? As described in the comment on 1:8, loyal action is spoken of within the context of a relationship between persons. What Ruth perceived as favor (2:10, 13), Naomi understands as loyalty, because Naomi knows of the relationship between her family and Boaz, while Ruth did not. Loyalty is life-saving action, generally done by one who is in a unique position to offer such help. The provision of food beyond the ordinary, offered by a wealthy member of the community who happens also to be a near relative, exemplifies such loyal behavior. To be sure, his action so far is limited, but already he has done more than was expected of him. Thus it is through Boaz that God's kindness to Naomi and Ruth receives its content and meaning. God had provided food for Judah (1:6), but only through Boaz has God provided food for the two returning widows. In God's providence Ruth came to Boaz's field, but it is Boaz who looks kindly upon Ruth in her need. Divine loyalty takes shape in the community and in individual lives through human actions.

One should not pass over Naomi's words of blessing without noting how radically her point of view has changed since her last extended speech at the end of chapter 1. There she spoke of God who had dealt bitterly with her, brought calamity upon her. Now she perceives that this same God has not abandoned kindness to her and her family. It would perhaps be claiming too much to suppose that Naomi has in this instant, upon hearing the mention of Boaz's name, completely reversed herself. To utter the thought that God has not forgotten after all does not mean the sudden erasure of all the pain of her loss, of having been brought back empty. The dead cannot be brought back to life or to Bethlehem. But if God has not forgotten them or her, then her relationship with God is different from what she had thought before. Every generation of Jews and Christians has struggled with the meaning of personal calamity. Every faithful person at some time has reason to ask, "why does it hurt so much?" Not all would agree with Naomi's assessment that God was the cause of her sorrow. Yet almost more important than assessing the cause is the realization that God does not abandon us in our suffering. In the words of the African-American community of struggle, God "helped them make a way out of no way" (Williams, p. 6). It is this realization that has come to Naomi as she hears Ruth's report; Naomi has begun a healing journey, a journey from despair to hope, a journey from a living death to a life worth living.

After her exclamation of blessing, Naomi goes on to explain to Ruth the relationship between Boaz and her family, describing him as "one of our nearest kin." Now (by contrast to 2:1) Boaz is identified as a gō'ēl, a word regularly used in the technical sense of a male relative

48

who has the right and responsibility to redeem (hence the alternative translation "redeemer") either the person or the land of one of his family members. The role of such a redeemer with regard to land is illustrated in the story of Jeremiah's purchase of the field of his cousin Hanamel (Jer. 32:6–15). Why Hanamel needed to sell is not known, but the purpose of the purchase was to prevent the land from being sold outside the family. In Jeremiah's context, the purchase serves a symbolic function. As the Babylonians are about to overrun the land, Jeremiah's purchase stands as a sign that ownership will matter again in the future; God promises that there is hope beyond the present crisis. Redemption of persons meant paying the necessary amount to prevent their being sold into slavery or to bring them back from servitude. Although we do not know enough about the kinship patterns in ancient Israel to identify the precise relationships that entailed such rights and responsibilities, maintaining the family unit and its possession of any inherited agrarian land were basic to the culture. The theme of the proper identity and responsibility of such a kinsman will be central to the following episodes of the story. Naomi has described Boaz as one among several such persons; she has also spoken of him to Ruth with the pronoun "our," thus including her foreign daughter-in-law within the circle of those for whom Boaz may have responsibility. Yet Naomi does not develop the significance she attaches to Boaz's redeemer status. Ruth and the reader are left to discover it as the story continues (see comment at 3:9b and 4:3–6).

Ruth now gives more details of her conversation with Boaz (v. 21). As she speaks of the instruction related to her safety, the narrator again refers to her as "the Moabite." There is an odd turn to her report that is obscured by the term "servants" in the NRSV translation. In Boaz's earlier instructions, distinction was made between young men and young women, masculine and feminine forms of the same word; Ruth was explicitly instructed to keep close to the young women. In her report to her mother-in-law, Ruth changes the object of the verb to the masculine form. While it could be that the masculine is used to encompass both genders, it is hard to understand why Ruth should so modify the words she is quoting. Possibly her focus is upon the time frame rather than the company—she is to do all her gleaning in Boaz's area during this harvest season, not move to the field of another. Implicit is the continuation of Boaz's instruction that she be given special privilege in order to gather more grain. This interpretation reinforces Boaz's act of kindness on behalf of Ruth the alien Moabite who is faithful daughter-in-law to Naomi, his relative by marriage.

Ruth's altered version of what Boaz had said also provides the occasion

49

for Naomi to express her own concern and to reiterate the same advice that Boaz had originally given. Although the NRSV translates "bother" in verse 22 as well as in verse 9 (see comment), Naomi uses a stronger Hebrew verb for the danger Ruth might face, a verb used elsewhere explicitly for violent action. The narrator now refers to Ruth not as the Moabite but as Naomi's daughter-in-law, returning the focus to their relationship.

The narrator concludes this section with the report that Ruth did as Naomi had instructed, "staying close" (the same verb used at 2:8 and 1:14; see comments there) to the young women in Boaz's field through the harvest. Thus chapter 2 ends in contrast to chapter 1; the two women are in harmony, Ruth no longer resisting the advice of her mother-in-law. The narrator mentions that Ruth lives with Naomi. We do not know whether gleaners usually slept elsewhere during the harvest. Whether or not Ruth's domicile was uncommon, the notice points the reader both back to Ruth's promise to lodge with Naomi and ahead to the night that Ruth will spend at the threshing floor.

The time of the barley harvest and the wheat harvest is April–May. Tradition associates the barley harvest with the period of Passover; the wheat harvest is marked by the Feast of Weeks, held seven weeks later. The transition from the beginning of the harvest season (1:22) to its end (2:23) hints at a routinization of Ruth's life as a gleaner. Progress of the story is suspended for a time; readers can catch their breath before the rapid and dramatic unfolding of events of chapters 3 and 4.

PART THREE

Seeking Security

RUTH 3

In broad strokes, the structural outline of chapter 3 parallels that of chapter 2. An opening section (vv. 1–5) of conversation between Naomi and Ruth is followed by a lengthier middle section (vv. 6–15) of encounter between Ruth and Boaz, with a brief concluding section (vv. 16–18) in which the two women discuss the events that have transpired outside the home. The effect of this broad parallel structure is heightened by certain internal elements set in contrast or in parallel to chapter 2. Most notably, the initiative in the opening section is Naomi's rather than Ruth's, and the initiative in the second section is Ruth's rather than Boaz's. While the middle section of each chapter concludes with Ruth bringing home food, the openings of these middle sections contrast a happenstance destination to a specifically planned one. Mention of the central thematic terms "faithfulness, loyalty" (*ḥesed*) and "next-of-kin, redeemer" (*gōʾēl*) moves from the lips of Naomi to those of Ruth and Boaz.

The determination of Naomi, the daring of Ruth, and the uprightness of Boaz that have already been exhibited are further illustrated in the behavior of the key characters in these scenes. Each shows concern for the welfare of another, yet the achieving of the other's welfare will take shape in a way that benefits the helper as well. Here, as in the preceding chapters, it is possible to read the story "against the grain," as Fewell and Gunn have proposed, to portray each character as primarily self-serving; but such a reading again requires a rejection or downplaying of motives explicitly expressed in the dialogue. Here, as earlier, it seems preferable to emphasize the expressed concern for others as the primary aspect of characterization by the storyteller, while still allowing for an undercurrent of human self-interest.

Ruth 3:1–5
Naomi and Ruth

Although the concluding verse of chapter 2 has given the impression of passage of time, the opening of this section still feels abrupt from a story-telling perspective. One misses some kind of transitional phrase such as "one day," or "some time later." The abruptness is not so disconcerting, however, when the opening is thought of as if reading a stage play. Readers have all the necessary background to follow the conversation.

Nonetheless, the time sequence of the narrative presents a seeming difficulty that has puzzled commentators. The last verse of chapter 1 dates the return of Ruth and Naomi to the beginning of the barley harvest. The last verse of chapter 2 moves time ahead not just to the end of the barley harvest, but also at least to the end of the wheat harvest, which follows directly upon the barley harvest. In 3:2, however, Naomi indicates that Boaz is at work winnowing *barley*. Efforts to read a different word here are speculative, and there is no evidence that the reference to the wheat harvest in 2:23 was a late addition. Apparently it was possible to delay winnowing of the first crop until the press of time for successful harvesting of the second crop had eased. In fact, the same sequence of back-to-back harvesting of barley and wheat persists in areas of the Middle East today. Traditional farmers have techniques for sealing the early harvest against weather, insects, and rodents for a number of weeks until the work schedule permits attention to threshing and winnowing. Although it cannot be known whether ancient Israelite villagers used the same techniques, the modern practice suggests that ancient hearers would have found the time sequence of the Ruth narrative quite plausible.

As chapter 3 opens, the storyteller places Naomi's role as mother-in-law in apposition to her name for the first and only time. Although Ruth's name is frequently specified by the terms Moabite or daughter-in-law, Naomi is everywhere else referred to either by her name or by her role, but not by both together. The exception helps to draw readers' attention to Naomi as the initiator of action, in contrast to her passive role in the opening part of chapter 2. It may also suggest that part of her role as mother-in-law in that culture was to see to the future of her son's widow. She has already made one effort in this direction by urging Ruth to join Orpah in remaining in Moab. Now that circumstances have greatly changed, she makes her second attempt.

That this is a second effort is made clear by Naomi's reference to "security," which she mentioned earlier in her first farewell speech (1:9). The single English term translates two very similar Hebrew terms derived from the same root. In chapter 1 Naomi expressed the hope that God would provide for Ruth the security of marriage that Naomi considered herself unable to provide. Now in the new situation that God has brought about through the loyal kindness of Ruth and the responding action of Boaz, Naomi herself develops a plan to arrange for this security, hoping to bring an end to the stopgap survival represented by gleaning.

Naomi reiterates two aspects of the women's relationship to Boaz already established in chapter 2. First, it is with Boaz's women servants that Ruth has been working, in accordance with instructions given both by Boaz and by Naomi and additionally confirmed by the narrator in concluding chapter 2. Second, Naomi again identifies Boaz as "our kinsman." The plural pronoun "our" that includes Ruth is reiterated from 2:20, but here yet a third Hebrew noun is employed to describe Boaz's relationship to them (cf. 2:1; 2:20). While it is not possible to identify all the nuances of this changing vocabulary, it seems likely that the terms refer to overlapping but not identical spheres of familial relationship and obligation. It is significant here that Naomi does *not* use the term *gō'ēl* in connection with her plan (see below on 3:9b).

Naomi says that Boaz will be winnowing barley, tossing the beaten-out grain in the air to remove the chaff. Given the presence of field workers in the earlier harvesting stage, it is not necessary to imagine that Boaz alone or even personally is involved in this task. The reference to eating and drinking (v. 3) suggests a day's or evening's communal work, followed by a meal, just as a mid-day meal involved all the workers in the field (2:14). The evening timing was probably dictated by the presence of the best breeze, neither too strong nor too light, which was necessary for the task at hand, and perhaps also by the scheduling of other agricultural duties.

Naomi instructs Ruth to bathe, to anoint her body, and to change her clothing. The significance of this series of preparatory actions has been debated. Some have suggested a parallel in Ezekiel 16:9–12, where Israel is pictured as a bride being prepared for her wedding by washing, anointing with oil, and dressing in special clothing. As Bush observes, however, the alleged parallel diverges at the critical point of the type of clothing mentioned (p. 151). In Ezekiel, special finery is clearly indicated, while Ruth 3:3 uses the ordinary Hebrew term for an

53

outer garment (so also Campbell, p. 120, who translates "cape"). Bush suggests that the series of actions should be interpreted as an ending of Ruth's period of mourning for her dead husband, by parallel to David's actions after the death of his infant son (II Sam. 12:20). This proposal is not compelling, however, since David took these steps not after a period of mourning for the dead child but immediately after the baby died, once his pleading for the life of the child had come to nought. Since the Hebrew word used in Ruth is a general one for clothing or outer garment, it seems that no special finery is in view (against "best clothes" of the NRSV and other modern translations). Yet it is still reasonable to suppose that Naomi wants Ruth to be attractive in every way for the proposed visit to the threshing floor. Bathing was probably not an everyday or even weekly practice in ancient Israel, and the use of oil (implied by the choice of the Hebrew verb "anoint") in such a non-utilitarian way as bodily anointing would surely have been even less frequent. So the introductory instructions for personal preparation already give Ruth a clue that Naomi has something unusual in mind.

That inkling is confirmed immediately as Naomi continues her instructions. Ruth is to approach Boaz at night, after he has finished eating and drinking, when he is lying down to sleep. She is further to lie down herself, and even "uncover his feet." If the implications of the preparatory toilette are ambiguous, these next instructions from Naomi are even more so. As one might expect, and as the concern to avoid detection (3:14) will make clear, a woman present with a man in a public area during the night, much less a woman lying next to a partially unclothed man under such circumstances, was far from customary or accepted practice. The term translated "feet" by the NRSV is not the usual word, but a less common synonym (appearing only in Ruth 3:4, 7, 8, 14; Dan. 10:6) better taken as "legs." Nonetheless, the possible connotation of genitalia, for which the ordinary word for feet is sometimes a euphemism, hovers near at hand. Likewise, the verb "to uncover" used here appears in idioms referring to sexual relations (e.g., Lev. 18:6ff.; Deut. 22:30 [Heb. 23:1]). The overtones of a possible sexual encounter are heard also in the verb to "lie down," which can mean literally to lie down, including lying down to "go to sleep," but also in certain constructions to "sleep with, have sexual relations with." The use of such vocabulary will continue in the next scene. Never is there any indication of the consummation of sexual relations, yet the choice of words keeps that possibility always before the reader. The storyteller creates an atmosphere of ambiguity and mystery (Campbell, pp. 131–32). In a story where so many customs and conventions have already been stretched, readers are led to wonder whether this time they will be stretched to the breaking point.

54

What is Naomi really suggesting? How will Ruth interpret these extraordinary instructions? How will she respond? Seeking Ruth's security, even in the form of marriage, may be a worthy goal on Naomi's part, but in such a manner, through such actions? Readers may well anticipate some objection from Ruth, or at least some request for clarification. But the expected response is not forthcoming. Ruth, who argued strenuously against Naomi's seemingly conventional proposal that she find her security in her Moabite homeland and family (chapter 1), now responds to a new and quite bizarre proposal with a simple sentence of compliance and cooperation: "All that you tell me I will do." As in so many places in this story, the reader is kept off balance by the characters' choices.

Although Ruth agrees to the plan, readers may still ask why Naomi herself devises such an approach. Why does Naomi not just go to Boaz herself and suggest that he marry Ruth? Or why not send Ruth to him under other, less compromising circumstances? A first answer, to be sure, is simply for reasons of good narrative art: the level of drama would be greatly diminished. As the interpretation of the next scene will suggest, the storyteller is able to use the nighttime encounter to maintain tension between the possibility of a sexual encounter and the possibility of reasoned planning for the future. Further, the factors of attractiveness and availability that are introduced may serve as a challenge to Boaz's lack of further initiative toward Ruth during the weeks of harvest following their initial encounter. Here the observations of Fewell and Gunn about the undercurrent of his personal attraction to Ruth in that scene should be kept in mind. Naomi's plan capitalizes on a possibility that is already in the air. Finally, it is easy to imagine that Naomi would expect to be rebuffed if she approached Boaz herself on Ruth's behalf. As will be seen in the interpretation of the next scene, his status as a *gō'ēl* does not place him under obligation of custom to marry Ruth, nor is she under such obligation to him. For Naomi to ask Boaz to marry her Moabite daughter-in-law might seem to him the height of foolishness. The occasion at the threshing floor, although fraught with great risk, will provide maximum opportunity for encouraging Boaz toward the desired goal.

Before leaving this scene, one must note that the theme of establishing women's security through marriage, especially through marriage to a prominent and wealthy man of the community, is highly problematic today. Although Ruth and Naomi may be models for women in their bonding together as women and in their working on their own to secure their survival, their story is set within an overarching and undergirding societal structure in which long-term security for women depends upon their being in relationship with some male who has access to economic assets. It is not by accident that Israelite tradition repeatedly groups the widow and orphan along with the poor as those neediest of the needy to whom society should offer protection. So it is that Ruth cooperates now with Naomi in seeking the marriage to Boaz. But it is just this fact, that the "happily ever after" of the story depends upon marriage, especially upon marriage to a rich man, that turns many modern readers away from appreciating the story, even causing some to view it as "dangerous to women's health" by lending scriptural authority to the "Cinderella" dream of the scullery maid winning the crown prince, a dream well inculcated into girl children even in modern western culture. A response to this and related difficulties is developed more fully in the Hermeneutical and Theological Postscript at the end of the commentary. To anticipate briefly, a text read in whatever respect as carrying an unhealthy message invites readers to work against replication of that message in their own societal contexts. Hermeneutically, it will be argued that the underlying societal vision of this story, not its particular form of enfleshment in Israel's particular ancient economic and family system, offers a proper and valuable basis for theological appropriation of the story.

Ruth 3:6–15
Ruth and Boaz

Initiating Contact (3:6–9a)

The scene shifts to the threshing floor with the narrator's summarizing, and at the same time anticipatory, comment that (as she had promised) Ruth follows Naomi's instructions. As expected, Boaz eats and drinks, then goes to lie down. The narrator observes that Boaz "was in a contented mood," offering one clue concerning Naomi's suggested timing for Ruth's action. The desire for a private encounter would of course also preclude any earlier timing. Now the narrator makes clearer that Boaz is lying down to sleep, not just to rest or for some other purpose: he is not aware of Ruth's arrival, uncovering of his legs, or lying down next to him.

Why Boaz awakens in the night has been the subject of considerable discussion by commentators. Some have found behind the verb "startle" or "shudder" a traditional fear of night demons, since the verb

56

is often associated with something fearful or threatening (e.g., Sasson, pp. 74–78); but others suggest that Boaz was just reacting to the chill of being without his usual covering (e.g., Campbell, p. 122; Trible, p. 183). Whatever the reason, Boaz is suddenly awake.

The sparseness of the narrative should not cause modern readers to miss Boaz's shock after awakening in the middle of the night to find himself partially uncovered and with a woman lying beside him (v. 8). One may readily imagine his reactions—am I dreaming? did I drink that much? have I forgotten something?—as he shakes himself more fully awake. For Boaz as the upright and prominent citizen of Bethlehem, the reality of the situation is not much improvement over any initial reactions he may have had, as is indicated by verse 14 near the end of the scene. His simple query, "Who are you?" may be heard in a tone that goes beyond information-gathering to convey surprise, uneasiness, perhaps fear and even anger.

Before reviewing the ensuing conversation between Ruth and Boaz, the ambiguity of the threshing floor scene, as well as its sparseness of information, should be reemphasized. This scene above all others entices readers toward imagination and speculation, if only because late-night encounters between a woman and a man are the most common cross-cultural feature of the story as a whole. Lacking textual controls, imagination may lead readers in wildly different directions: a steamy tryst between mutually desiring persons (in the genre of the North American soap opera or formulaic romance novel); or, a beautiful but needy young Ruth forcing herself to relate to a rough, pot-bellied, snaggle-toothed (but rich) old man for the sake of her mother-in-law; or, a wily, scheming Ruth cooperating with Naomi to compromise and thus force the hand of the most handsome and wealthy bachelor of the community. The very reticence of the text leads readers to supply additional details; the three suggestions just outlined come from actual conversations about the text and are to some degree represented in the published literature. Awareness of competing interpretations by other readers challenges each reader to greater self-awareness and greater attention to what limited evidence is provided by the text itself.

Ruth's Words (3:9b)

To Boaz's shocked inquiry, Ruth must give reply. At this point the encounter moves beyond the range of Naomi's instructions, for she had told Ruth only what to do, not what to say. By opening with a question rather than by telling Ruth what to do, Boaz has moved the encounter away from Naomi's anticipated scenario (v. 4). Ruth's reply begins, normally enough, by announcing her name; then she adds, again as would be expected, a term indicating her status in relation to Boaz. The Hebrew term she uses (NRSV "your servant") is not, however, the same term that she used in their previous conversation in the harvesting fields (2:13, also "your servant" in NRSV). Some scholars view the two Hebrew terms as simple synonyms, and the NRSV follows this tradition by its use of the same English word in both cases. Others, however, regard the distinction as significant, interpreting Ruth's usage in 2:13 as a general term for female slave, but the new term in 3:9 as a specific indication of her availability as a wife or concubine for a man who is not himself a slave (Sasson pp. 53–54, 81). Berlin's literary analysis sees a definite upward progression in Ruth's status here (pp. 88, 152 n. 5), but Steinberg's anthropological analysis is suspicious of such fine tuning (p. 63 n. 55). Literary arguments stand in tension with anthropological ones, and comparisons between usage in Ruth and in equally disputed texts such as Genesis 16 (Sarah and Hagar) and I Samuel 25 (David and Abigail) further compound the difficulty. It is difficult to draw a sure conclusion from such mixed evidence.

Whether or not Ruth is hinting at a different perspective on her status by this different self-identification, her next words make quite clear that she has in mind a change in the relationship between herself and Boaz. She does not cease speaking after answering his question, but goes on to give him a specific instruction: "spread your cloak over your servant." Although her language is symbolic, even veiled, its reference to marriage would be clear to the ancient Israelite hearer. The term translated "cloak" by the NRSV is literally in Hebrew "wing," as in the wing of a bird; a secondary meaning relates to the loose flowing end of a garment. Ruth's choice of this term is charged with significance in two respects. First, the idiom to cover with the wing/garment is not an ordinary request for warmth, but refers to the establishing of a marriage bond. The idiom appears elsewhere in the Hebrew Bible in Ezekiel 16:8, where the phrasing is most closely parallel; related usage appears in Deuteronomy 22:30 [Heb 23:1]; 27:20. There is ancient Near Eastern evidence for the symbolic use of a man's garment hem in divorce proceedings (Kruger, pp. 79–86).

In the overall context of the story of Ruth, the use of this terminology to suggest marriage has yet another level of symbolic meaning, for the term "wing" has appeared earlier (2:12) on the lips of Boaz as he spoke of God's wings under which Ruth has sought refuge. Now Ruth in effect invites Boaz to make good on the prayer he made earlier on her behalf, by providing some measure of the "full reward" of refuge under God's wings through his own action, by marrying her. Again a central theme of the book appears, namely that human action is the vehicle for achieving divine blessing and the fullness of human community. Ruth hoped to "continue to find favor" in the sight of Boaz (2:13); if he takes this huge next step beyond a generous and protected gleaning opportunity, her refuge in the God of Israel will be more secure.

Why should Boaz marry Ruth? Not because she has compromised him by appearing near him or uncovering him in the night, for this is witnessed by no one, known to no one else except Naomi. Not because Boaz is attracted to her in any case; this may be true but is at best an undercurrent of the story as it is told. The reason Ruth gives, "for you are next-of-kin," seems at first straightforward but raises a host of questions. The Hebrew term underlying "next-of-kin" here is *gō'ēl* (also translated "redeemer"), the same word used by Naomi in 2:20 but not in 3:2. The word is a participial form of the verb meaning "to act as next of kin" in the sense of "to redeem"; kinship and specific responsibilities are here closely intertwined. For instance, in certain Hebrew laws the next-of-kin has a right and responsibility to purchase back (redeem) a piece of property that is about to go outside the family (Lev. 25:25–28; cf. Jer. 32:6–15 and comment at 2:20 above), or within limits to seek blood vengeance for the murdered relative (Num. 35:12), or to purchase back a relative who has sold himself because of financial difficulty to a resident alien (Lev. 25:47–50). The term is a legal one, but it is highly charged socially because it focuses on the preservation of family and community. And yet, there is a glaring gap between the appearance of the word *gō'ēl* in Ruth 3:9b and its technical usage elsewhere in the Old Testament: nowhere else is the term *gō'ēl* associated with rights or responsibilities pertaining to marriage. The regulation having to do with rights and responsibilities in cases where a man is to marry his brother's widow to perpetuate the family line is the law of levirate marriage, found in Deuteronomy 25:5–10 and illustrated in the story of Tamar, Genesis 38; but the levirate provisions contain no reference to the *gō'ēl*. Only in the book of Ruth do the two spheres of marriage among kin and land redemption among kin seem to come together.

Most scholars believe that both of these customs are at work in chapter 4, where the question of the dead man's name (levirate marriage) arises along with the question of redemption of a parcel of land, and most try to import both into the interpretation of Ruth's statement here in chapter 3 and into Boaz's subsequent reply. For at least three reasons, the relationship (if any) between the two customs is difficult to perceive even in chapter 4: first, adequate knowledge of the ancient practices is lacking; second, biblical "laws" represent only sample

59

guides in the form of case precedents, not formal statutes in the modern Western sense of enacted legislation; and third, it is quite possible that both customs varied over time, but we are unable to establish an exact chronology of even our limited examples of legal and narrative texts. The attempt to introduce the concept of levirate marriage as a presupposition of chapter 3 multiplies interpretive difficulties, particularly with regard to understanding the first and last instances of Ruth's loyalty (v. 10). Bush's recent work has effectively laid out many of the problems of earlier treatments (including my own in *The Meaning of Hesed*, pp. 42–43); the broad contours of his proposal for understanding the uses of the root *g'l* in this passage will be followed here.

How is it then, that the storyteller seems to have no difficulty with the connection Ruth makes between her marriage proposal and Boaz's status as *gō'ēl*? As Bush suggests, Ruth's rationale "because you are next-of-kin/redeemer" does not have in mind the specific legal connotations pertaining to *gō'ēl* in its technical usage. Rather, she uses the term in a more general sense, which can plausibly be deduced from Naomi's words in 2:20. Boaz is one of a group of kinsmen who has responsibility for the well-being of Naomi, and by extension for her daughter-in-law. The goal of the marriage in Ruth's mind is familial and economic security. It is not related to any unmentioned land deal (*gō'ēl* in a technical legal sense, cf. chapter 4), nor is its intention to produce an heir for her dead husband Mahlon (levirate marriage). Although Campbell treats Ruth's reference to the redeemer differently, relating it directly to levirate practice, he expresses eloquently the basic function of the *gō'ēl*:

> Redeemers . . . are to take responsibility for the unfortunate and stand as their supporters and advocates. They are to embody the basic principle of caring responsibility for those who may not have justice done for them by the unscrupulous, or even by the person who lives by the letter of the law (p. 136).

It is this general notion that Ruth reflects in her words to Boaz.

The frequent Old Testament use of redemption language with reference to God further heightens, albeit indirectly, the significance of Ruth's description of Boaz as next-of-kin/redeemer. Israel's hymns speak of God's redemption of Israel from bondage in Egypt (e.g., Ps. 77:15 [Heb. v. 16]; Exod. 15:13); the prophet Deutero-Isaiah repeatedly portrays God as Redeemer of Israel from Babylonian exile (e.g., Isa. 43:1; 44:6; 48:20). Closer thematically to the Ruth narrative, God is remembered as the Redeemer of individuals, the One who is in relationship with them, supports them, and rescues them from desperate circumstances (e.g., Ps. 103:4; 69:18 [Heb. v. 19]; Prov. 23:11). In such texts, the metaphorical language resonates most closely with the basic function of the redeemer as described by Campbell. It is the redemptive action of God that provides the standard for human acts of redemption, even as awareness of such human behavior provides an entry point for imagining a God who takes human needs so seriously. In the story of Ruth, where God is largely behind the scene, the role of a human redeemer becomes crucial.

In sum, this interpretation of Ruth's use of the word "next-of-kin/redeemer" avoids both the category of land redemption and the category of levirate marriage. It thus makes narrative sense of her suggestion of marriage apart from any reference or even indirect allusion either to property or to offspring. It further makes narrative sense in that it does not presuppose that Ruth has technical knowledge of Israelite laws or customs. Boaz will subsequently build a more elaborate technical plan upon Ruth's general use of the word. Finally, her general use of the term picks up on the central motif of the story as a whole, namely, human protection and support as a manifestation of God's redemptive care.

Boaz's Reply (3:10–13)

Remarkably, Boaz is immediately appreciative of what Ruth has done and said. Again addressing her as "my daughter" (cf. 2:8), he invokes divine blessing upon her because "this last instance of your loyalty is better than the first." The phrase "instance of loyalty" represents the crucial Hebrew term *hesed,* discussed above at 1:8b and 2:20. Boaz is praising Ruth for acts done in relationship, essential acts of support and caring that only she was in a position to accomplish, acts that frequently go beyond the basic call of duty. It is generally agreed that Ruth's "first" act of loyalty was her accompanying Naomi and caring for her by gleaning in Bethlehem, while the "last" act is her coming to the threshing floor and proposing the marriage. But in what sense can her proposal of marriage be viewed as a "better" or greater act? Looking to Boaz rather than to some younger man of the village as a marriage partner (v. 10b) at first glance hardly seems as great an act of loyalty as the commitment to Naomi. Yet the comment about the young men reveals that Ruth was not regarded as under legal obligation to marry a relative of her dead husband within the rules of levirate marriage. Her willingness to marry Boaz goes beyond the call of duty; clearly the marriage will ensure Naomi's security, not just her own. Thus it is an act of loyalty, greater because it provides for long-range security beyond the short-term solution of gleaning and greater because it clarifies the depth of Ruth's

61

commitment to the promises she made to Naomi, since the marriage will make permanent Ruth's bond to Naomi's place and people.

As Boaz continues to speak, his words of comfort ("do not be afraid") remind readers how great a risk Ruth has taken in approaching him by night and in making her proposal. How easily he could have taken advantage of her physically. How easily he could have rebuffed her proposal. How easily he could have compromised her integrity, letting the village know what had happened and giving his own interpretation of the event. Trible rightly entitles the encounter "salvation by courage alone" (p. 181).

Boaz's agreement to Ruth's request and his assertion of her good reputation confirm his awareness of her reasons to be afraid. His description of Ruth's reputation in the community as a "worthy woman" (*'ēšet ḥayil*) calls to mind another appearance of this rare phrase in the introduction to the classic description of the kind of woman to be desired as a wife (Prov. 31:10; NRSV "capable wife"). Although Ruth is not at this point wealthy or married with children (cf. Prov. 31:22, 28), the overall theme of the woman who takes initiative inside and outside the household arena to provide for her family is remarkably appropriate to the Ruth portrayed in the book thus far. She does good, not harm (see Prov. 31:12); she "works with willing hands" (31:13) and "provides food for her household" (31:15); "strength and dignity are her clothing" (31:25); "the teaching of kindness (*ḥesed*) is on her tongue" (31:26); she "does not eat the bread of idleness" (31:27); she "fears the LORD" (31:30). The possibility of inter-textual allusion to Proverbs 31 is strengthened by the presence of a second unusual expression used in this same sentence with *'ēšet ḥayil*. The NRSV phrase "all the assembly of my people" is more literally translated "all the gate of my people." Although its technical meaning is debated, this expression calls to mind the concluding phrase from the lengthy description of the capable wife: "let her works praise her in the city gates" (Prov. 31:31). It is easy to imagine, based on what is known of Ruth so far, that as Boaz's wife she would become the epitome of the wife described in Proverbs. But it is equally important to emphasize that so many key traits of a "worthy woman" are recognizable in Ruth quite apart from the context of marriage, children, and wealth presupposed in Proverbs 31. Her story thus serves as a balance and corrective to any cultural assumption that only married women are truly "worthy."

Boaz's use of the expression "worthy woman" is of further significance in its function as a feminine counterpart to the narrator's opening description of Boaz in 2:1 as *gibbôr ḥayil* (NRSV "prominent rich man"). While Ruth is neither prominent nor rich, the appearance of the parallel expression collapses the social distance between them, while at the same time suggesting that Boaz is not only prominent and rich, but is also to be thought of as morally worthy, one whose uprightness, fear of God, and diligence on behalf of family are admired in the community. This picture of Boaz has begun already to emerge in the events subsequent to 2:1 and will be fully confirmed by the end of the story.

As Boaz's lengthy reply continues in verses 12–13, he picks up on Ruth's use of the next-of-kin/redeemer terminology in a way that moves quickly beyond her general meaning in the direction of more technical legal usage. Boaz uses the Hebrew root no less than five times, twice in the participial noun form in verse 12, then three times in verbal constructions in verse 13. His concern for the rank ordering of kinsmen ("there is another kinsman more closely related than I") and his insistence that this other man be given first option to exercise the right of the next-of-kin clearly fits within a legal rather than a general frame of reference. From the viewpoint of the story line as a whole, Boaz is able to consider Ruth's words in a larger context, anticipating consequences well beyond those she had in mind as she approached the threshing floor. His more technical use of redemption terminology points ahead to the next morning, when he will introduce the issue of control of a parcel of land (4:3).

Because he is aware of the larger implications of Ruth's marriage, Boaz recognizes that Ruth's last act of loyalty for Naomi (the proposed marriage) will yield even greater benefits than Ruth herself anticipates. No wonder he has invoked blessing upon her; no wonder he has spoken of her reputation as a "worthy woman." As Naomi's words earlier (2:20) provided the clue that Ruth had done more for Naomi (and, to be sure, for herself) than she realized by coming to the fields of Boaz, so here Boaz's use of redemption terminology provides the clue that Ruth's action will once again bear unexpected fruit. If God's providential guidance lies behind the scene in chapter 2 (see comment at 2:1), perhaps it is equally appropriate to think of God's redemptive activity behind this scene in chapter 3. God's redemption of the least of the least in Bethlehem is initiated by Ruth's act of *ḥesed* in approaching Boaz; that redemption will likewise come to fruition through the response of a human redeemer.

Into his remarks about the situation concerning the next-of-kin, Boaz introduces two instructions to Ruth regarding her most immediate action. Verse 13 begins with "remain this night" and concludes with "lie down until the morning." Why this double instruction, and why the risky (so it would seem) course of action that prolongs the nocturnal encounter? Each of his two phrases reintroduces a verb freighted with significance from earlier in the narrative. The first, NRSV "remain," is the same verb "to lodge" that Ruth used in her words of commitment to Naomi (1:16). Surely this is not accidental within the overall artistry of

63

the storyteller. Although the expression Boaz uses is a common one for "spending the night," Ruth's "lodging" with Boaz this night anticipates her lodging with him after their marriage. Yet the marriage will not mean a diminishing of the commitment to "lodge" with Naomi; quite the contrary, Ruth's relationship with Naomi, as suggested above, will be made more solid and permanent through marriage to one of Naomi's kinsmen.

Boaz's second instruction in effect specifies how Ruth is to spend the remainder of the night with him. The verb is the same as that used by Naomi (v. 4) and the narrator (vv. 7–8) to describe the situation of Boaz and Ruth before this fateful conversation. She is to lie down, perhaps also with the sense of "going to sleep" (see above); again the simple instruction steers well clear of sexual activity, while still reminding hearers of what could have been. The reason for prolonging Ruth's stay can only be guessed at. The usual proposal is that Boaz wanted to avoid any danger to Ruth that might have arisen from her moving about at night. The suggestion is plausible and focuses on Boaz's uprightness, but it might also be that Boaz here takes into account his own pleasure in having Ruth near at hand. After all, who knows what the next-of-kin will decide to do in the morning; this may be his last as well as his first private time with Ruth. Whatever the reason(s), the narrative effect of Ruth's presence throughout the night continues the mystery and ambiguity of the scene that the storyteller has so carefully crafted.

Departure (3:14–15)

The narrator amplifies Ruth's obedience to Boaz's instruction to "lie down until morning" with the additional specification of "at his legs [NRSV feet]," using the same term for the lower body area that Ruth had previously uncovered. Thus the mystery of the balance between sexual attraction and upright behavior is brought full circle. Although the term "morning" most often is associated with the arrival of daylight, Ruth's departure takes place before dawn, just as the deepest night begins to lift, at a time when a human figure can be discerned but not individually identified. It seems possible to assume that at this hour others might be making an early start toward their duties, so that her movements once she gained some distance from the threshing floor would not be a cause for surprise or alarm. Boaz does not want it known that this particular woman had been at this particular place (v. 14b). Why Boaz expresses this concern so belatedly (the Hebrew lacks the causal "for" supplied by the NRSV) and does not address it directly to Ruth (speaking instead of "the woman") has troubled translators since ancient times; all solutions require multiple emendations and do not substantially change the sense of what took place.

Before her departure, Boaz provides Ruth with a gift of barley, presumably from the just-winnowed pile of grain. Although the exact amount cannot be determined (the size of the measure is not specified), it is most likely a substantial amount. The purpose of the gift is revealed only in the next scene, when Ruth rejoins Naomi. Boaz himself loads the grain-filled garment onto Ruth's back, perhaps because of its weight, perhaps as a gesture of tenderness, since it is the closest to physical contact between the two that the narrator makes explicit. The narrator draws the episode quickly to a close with the report that "he entered the city" (i.e., Bethlehem).

At this point a number of Hebrew manuscripts and ancient versions read instead that "she (i.e., Ruth) entered the city"; many modern translations and commentators follow this alternative ending to the scene. Either reading is plausible, and this is probably a case of ancient variant traditions. An ending referring to Ruth creates a pleasing rounding-off of the overall focus on her departure in these verses; it also provides a nice combination of contrast and parallel with her departure from the gleaning field in 2:18, in which she herself picked up the barley that she had gleaned and then "entered the city" (the Hebrew phrase is the same, despite the different NRSV translation at 2:18).

Ruth 3:16–18
Naomi and Ruth

In a brief but significant scene, Ruth reports what has transpired and Naomi evaluates the situation and gives further advice. To Naomi's eager question, the storyteller allows the narrator to supply most of the reply under the rubric "all that the man had done for her." Contrary to Trible's interpretation (pp. 186–87), there is no need to suppose that Ruth may have withheld information about her conversation with Boaz; Naomi's reply (v. 18) indicates a full understanding of the situation. Rather, the summary is intended to move the reader's attention quickly to the quotation from Boaz (v. 17b), which supplies additional information not known from the previous scene.

Rhetorically and narratively, what is central to the report about the meeting at the threshing floor is not that Boaz agreed to the plan for Ruth's marriage, but rather what is revealed in v. 17b: Boaz is concerned to provide for Naomi. The term for "empty-handed" that Ruth attributes to Boaz is the same that Naomi used earlier in asserting that the LORD had brought her back "empty" from Moab to Bethlehem (1:21). Surely

65

the storyteller's repetition of the term is not accidental. Since these words of Boaz were not reported earlier, Berlin suggests (p. 98) that Ruth's report reflects what she thought was Boaz's intention, not what he actually had said himself. The thread of the story is more powerful, however, if Ruth's report is taken at face value as Boaz's actual words. Boaz's explanation of his gift of grain provides a sure clue that he joins Ruth in her concern for Naomi; he is not focused on Ruth alone. At the very least, Naomi will be physically "full" (1:21), and this fullness may anticipate fullness of life in other respects. Indeed, one might look back and suppose that Boaz's arrangements for extra sheaves and his surplus midday meal provisions in the gleaning fields (2:14, 16) were also intended to ensure that Ruth not come to her mother-in-law "empty," although the reason then was never spoken. Because Naomi is told Boaz's words about her, she herself as well as readers of the story may look hopefully toward an ending in which Boaz shows as much concern for Naomi's well-being as does the loyal Ruth.

Naomi concludes the scene with an expression of confidence in Boaz's prompt and appropriate action. Perhaps her "wait, my daughter, until you learn . . . " should be read as a gentle word of caution to Ruth, who may not have taken the legal ramifications of an unknown and unidentified nearer kinsman with sufficient seriousness. Naomi, Ruth, and the readers await developments over which the women can have no control.

From this point forward in the story, the voices of Ruth and Naomi are heard no more. Their speaking parts end at the point where each has done whatever she can to assure a good future for the other. As the first words of Naomi (1:8–9) and of Ruth (1:16) were focused on the welfare of the other, so also their words in this final exchange have lifted up that same focus. In the first exchange, however, no outside support was on the horizon of the widows' world; but now both women speak of the man who has promised that Ruth's security and Naomi's fullness will be provided for and that the role of redeemer will be fulfilled. Their future lies in the hands of this man; how fortunate that he has grounded his promise in an oath ("as the LORD lives," 3:13) by the name of the God who is Redeemer par excellence of the widow and the poor.

PART FOUR

The Peaceable Community

RUTH 4

The final chapter of the story begins in the public setting of the town gate with a primarily if not completely male constituency (vv. 1–12), moves briefly inward to the privacy of Boaz and Ruth's conjugal bed and the birth of Ruth's child (v. 13), then moves outward again to the community of women who had first greeted Naomi upon her return to Bethlehem (vv. 14–17). A postscript (vv. 18–22) elaborates the genealogy of King David, through whose prominence Ruth's own story is accorded greater prominence in the Israelite community.

In the course of events the transformation from emptiness to fullness, from sorrow to joy, from death to life, anticipated by God's gift of food (1:6) and Boaz's gifts of grain (2:14–16; 3:15), comes to rich and overflowing fruition. A broken family is reestablished, a marginalized outsider is brought into the community circle, a new life comes into the world, the atmosphere is permeated with blessing and rejoicing.

Yet this foretaste of God's promised future, of the peaceable kingdom in the microcosmic form of a single village as a peaceable community, includes features and comes about by processes that many readers in today's communities of faith find objectionable. Among other criticisms, readers have observed that men alone make decisions, women's property rights are doubtful, marriage and motherhood are idealized as women's proper role in the community, responsibility for a baby's nurture is transferred so as to undercut maternal prerogative. How Israel's picture of a "happy ending" may be understood theologically in the face of such objections is considered in the Hermeneutical and Theological Postscript to the commentary, as well as in the Introduction.

67

Ruth 4:1–12
At the Town Gate

Chapter 3 concluded with Ruth and Naomi waiting at home, anticipating some resolution from the action Boaz has promised to take. The scene now shifts to the gate, understood from context to be the town gate of Bethlehem. Juridical proceedings in Israel are often described as taking place at the gate of a town (e.g., Deut. 21:19; 22:15; Isa. 29:21; Amos 5:15); presumably an open public area adjacent to the gate is intended. One practical reason for such a location is apparent from the opening of this scene: many people would pass by en route to work in the fields or other business, so the opportunity to gather those needed for any decision-making would be easier.

Assembling the Participants (4:1–2)

Although the events to transpire at the town gate involve Naomi and Ruth explicitly and directly, neither woman will be present, much less have a voice. Boaz now takes center stage, following through on his oath before the LORD (3:13). Boaz goes to the gate and takes a seat, and just at the opportune moment the closer next-of-kin comes walking by. The Hebrew expression used by the narrator matches that used for the opportune arrival of Boaz in his field while Ruth is gleaning (2:4), another clue to readers that divine providence is at work, and thus that a favorable outcome may be expected. Boaz invites the nearer kinsman to sit also; the location, the choice of a more emphatic imperative verb form, and perhaps Boaz's tone of voice surely provided the next-of-kin an indication that this was to become a formal proceeding, not just a private chat. Oddly, Boaz does not address this man by a personal name, but rather with the vague and neutral phrase "so and so" (see translations by Campbell and Bush; NRSV "friend" is overly interpretive). It seems highly improbable, even impossible, that Boaz actually would not have known the name of this person, since he knew exactly how the man fit into a particular sequence of extended family relations. The question thus becomes a literary one. Does the storyteller want us to believe that Boaz really addressed the nearer kinsman without using his name? Or has the storyteller used the expression "so and so" for some rhetorical purpose, to avoid supplying the personal name that Boaz would have

68

used? In either case, the effect is a subtle devaluation of the unnamed character; he will move on and off the stage with even less identity than Orpah, who is his structural counterpart in the overall literary design of the story. That is not to say that he is criticized for not claiming his role as redeemer, any more than Orpah is criticized for obeying Naomi's instruction and returning to her family. But the actions of these minor characters serve as contrasts to highlight the "more excellent way" chosen by Ruth and by Boaz.

With the other principal party now present, Boaz assembles a group of ten elders, apparently the number needed before the proceeding can begin. Again, our knowledge of customs surrounding such proceedings is greatly lacking. From this narrative it appears that the term "elder" applied to some but not all of the males in the town, and that there were more than ten of them. Whether Boaz selected ten from a larger pool present at the gate or whether he simply called over the first ten who passed by (using the same imperative verb with which he had addressed the next-of-kin) cannot be determined. It does seem clear that the function of these ten is to be official witnesses, rather than to take any part in the action itself. Thus it would not be prejudicial to the outcome that they are all invited by Boaz himself.

The range of participation in the witnessing of the transaction expands as the narrative proceeds, perhaps for rhetorical effect. Boaz first seats these ten; then in his opening explanation of the case he speaks of the transaction taking place "in the presence of those sitting here, and in the presence of the elders of my people" (v. 4); finally, at the conclusion of the transaction it is "all the people who were at the gate, along with the elders" who voice their official word of witness (v. 11). This change, with its subtle three-step increase in the number of people giving attention to what is taking place, signals the importance of the decision for the entire community and the investment of all its members in the outcome. Interest in the proceedings may be attributed partly to the excitement of a potential marriage between a rich community leader and a poor, widowed foreigner (a Moabite woman, no less); but underlying that natural curiosity is the theological reality that the fate of one foreign woman and the fate of one impoverished widow's land do indeed matter enormously for the wholeness of the Bethlehem community. What vision of God's gracious rule will be embodied in the outcome of this event? The fact that the ancestry of King David is at stake, although this is known only to the narrator, further underscores the importance of this moment for every Bethlehemite, as they represent in microcosm the whole people of God.

69

The Transaction (4:3–6)

With the ten elders seated, Boaz initiates the proceedings. The preparatory steps in verses 1–2 have already left scholars with uncertainties about Israel's legal procedure. Now the actual conversation between Boaz and the next-of-kin raises vastly more difficult questions about the Israelite customs and the legal and moral rights and obligations presumed in this exchange. The problems are multiple and interlocking. They involve decisions about very technical grammatical and syntactical matters, choices about common versus rare (even otherwise unattested) connotations of common Hebrew verbs such as "buy" and "sell," as well as theories about practices of land tenure and inheritance, about sale of land and redemption rights, and about marriage practices in cases of a man's death without male offspring. So interlocked are the problems here, and so full of uncertainties, that the literature on the topic may fairly be described as chaotic, with no two scholars in significant agreement with each other over the full range of issues. Bush devotes nearly forty pages (pp. 196–233) of the technical section of his commentary to a summary and assessment of the debate over these four verses; readers may consult his work for a fuller description and analysis of the issues at stake. Here the presentation will be restricted to brief identification of the major difficulties and their consequences for interpreting the story.

The many proposals for understanding these verses generally begin from the appropriate assumption that what we have received from the hand of the storyteller made sense to the writer and to the original audience, however unclear it may be to us. A further assumption put forward by many interpreters, and with which I concur, is that we are dealing with a competent, indeed talented storyteller, whose story would not have been difficult for those original hearers to follow. If one approaches the conversation at the town gate with these assumptions, several key questions readily present themselves to "naive" modern readers.

First, how is it that Naomi has control over her dead husband's land so that she can "sell" it? How did she acquire that control? Why are she and Ruth pictured as impoverished (so that Ruth must go out gleaning) if Naomi owns a piece of land? And by what authority is Boaz announcing what Naomi intends to do about the land?

Second, what is at stake in the offer to the nearer kinsman of the opportunity to redeem the parcel of land? What is the balance between rights and duties in this situation? Should we here speak of his "right" if it is to his personal advantage (economic or otherwise) to take up the offer, but his "duty" if it is in some respect to his disadvantage to redeem the land? Is this a legal or a moral obligation? What will it cost him?

Third, why is "acquiring Ruth" connected to the redemption of the land? Which is the more likely meaning of the Hebrew text of verse 5: that the next-of-kin acquires Ruth at the same time as he redeems the parcel of land, or that Boaz acquires Ruth in any case? Assuming with the NRSV and nearly all commentators that it is the next-of-kin who would acquire Ruth, is Boaz stating a legal fact, or a right, or a legal or a moral obligation? Does the double use of "acquire" in verse 5 reduce Ruth's personhood by treating her as property to be purchased? What combination of answers to these questions makes the most sense of the change of mind on the part of the next-of-kin, and what combination makes at the same time reasonable sense in terms of our limited knowledge of land tenure and marriage practices from other biblical and ancient Near Eastern texts?

The starting point for understanding Naomi's situation with regard to Elimelech's land must be the biblical perspective that all the land belonged to its giver, God, and was held in trust by members of the community. A variety of traditions, from the insistence in Numbers 36 that land must not move from tribe to tribe, to the narratives of parceling out of the land in the book of Joshua, to the provisions for the Jubilee year restoration of land to its original "owners" (Leviticus 25), suggest that the possession of land was carefully tracked and that there were constraints on its transfer.

Although there is no indication in the biblical collections of legal precedents (case laws) that a widow could inherit property, it is evident (given the assumptions stated above) that Naomi has some claim with respect to Elimelech's land, whether to the property itself or to the usufruct (the right to use the produce of the land). One possibility for interpreting the situation is that Elimelech sold either the land or the right to use its produce before departing for Moab; Naomi now has the right to buy back what was sold but cannot afford to do so. What she is "selling" is that right of repurchase, and a redeemer is needed who will pay to keep it in the family. Alternatively, Elimelech may have made no arrangement concerning the disposition of his land, since the land was not producing during the famine and he perhaps expected to make a speedy return to Bethlehem once conditions improved. In this case, Naomi may have the right to the land since Elimelech has left no heir; but for some reason (recognizable to the ancient reader but not to us) she cannot simply take it back from whoever has farmed it in the intervening ten or more years. In this case also, she would be "selling" her right to retrieve what could be hers; again it is her poverty that requires the intervention of a redeemer so that the property is not permanently let go.

Why does Boaz raise this matter, as if out of nowhere? The storyteller gives no indication of any conversation about the topic between

71

the characters up to this point, and the artistry of the story overall suggests that readers should not have to posit such a missing scene in order to make sense of what is happening. The comments on 3:12–13 above proposed that Boaz's more technical use of redeemer terminology in his reply to Ruth anticipates his introducing here of the issue of land, with which redemption is primarily associated in extant case law. One may speculate that the question of transfer of land rights could not be broached during the harvest season, when the question of rights to the produce of many months' labor would be so immediate. In that case, this post-harvest moment is the earliest time since Naomi's arrival that the subject could be dealt with in the community. It is also possible (and not incompatible with the former suggestion) that Boaz has thought of an ingenious way to tie together the decision about Ruth's marriage (the only concern raised by Ruth at the threshing floor) with the matter of land tenure left unresolved by the death of Elimelech and his sons. In that case, the ancient hearer is surely at this point admiring Boaz for his cleverness, even as we remain puzzled about the precise confluence of opportunity and obligation that make his plan effective.

The nearer kinsman agrees to redeem Naomi's field until Boaz states by way of follow-up that the kinsman will be "also acquiring Ruth . . ." At that point the kinsman reverses himself, stating that the transaction would damage his own inheritance. It is surely not accidental that Boaz here identifies Ruth as "the Moabite, the widow of the dead man" and states the purpose of the marriage as "to maintain the dead man's name on his inheritance." The comment on 3:10 above pointed out that Ruth was not under obligation to remarry in such manner as to preserve the name (memory, lineage) of her dead husband. Yet it appears that the culture must presume at least a moral, if not a legal, obligation of a male relative to offer to take her in marriage for this purpose. The precise level of this obligation may have depended upon various factors, including the distance of the relationship between the kinsman and the dead man, the current circumstances of the kinsman, and the wishes of the surviving widow. The story of Tamar (Genesis 38) and the levirate regulation (Deut. 25:5–10) refer to such circumstances, but the two texts diverge from each other and from Ruth in significant details. The theme of maintaining a man's name on his inheritance (i.e., his parcel of land) is paralleled most closely in Numbers 27 and 36, which together allow a daughter (in the absence of sons) to receive her father's inheritance, with the proviso that she must marry within her own clan; but again there are significant differences from Ruth 4.

72

One possible scenario for understanding the situation in Ruth is as follows: Through redemption the kinsman would obtain rights to

Naomi's (i.e., Elimelech's) land and/or the use of its produce. The land would thus stay in the extended family; the redeemer would have some obligation to support Naomi and/or to allow her to reacquire the property from him if her circumstances ever allowed. Although the kinsman would have to pay for the land redemption, he might benefit in the long run, or at least not be worse off. He is willing to fulfill his legal obligation in this regard. But then he is confronted by Boaz with a further moral (not necessarily legal) obligation on behalf of the men who have died: he should marry Ruth, with the possibility of the birth of a son in view. Somehow (although we cannot reconstruct the inheritance regulations) the anticipated son would have rights to the redeemed parcel of land with no further payment required, so that the kinsman would eventually lose his investment.

A scenario such as this places the nearer kinsman in a position where the pressure of public opinion in the gate is brought to bear. If he accepts the legal right of redemption (potentially to his economic advantage) without accepting as well the moral obligation of marriage (potentially to his economic disadvantage), he will lose respect in the community. In his statement about his change of position, the nearer kinsman collapses the two aspects of Boaz's proposal. Since the redemption of land must involve the marriage also, he cannot take on the first without disadvantaging his own future. (Perhaps he hesitated also at the thought of marrying a Moabite, but the economic reason is the only point verbalized.) He therefore relinquishes both the legal right and the moral obligation, each of which is then assumed by Boaz.

Finally, although Boaz uses the verb "to acquire" (Hebrew *qnh*) both for the land to be redeemed and for the woman to be married (v. 5), it should not be concluded that Ruth or Israelite wives in general are regarded merely as "property." Several points tell against such an interpretation. First, the use of this verb in connection with marriage is unique to this passage. Thus the verb should not be used as a basis for hypothesizing about Israelite attitudes toward marriage in general; to the contrary, its uniqueness in contrast to more usual idioms suggests that a special point is being made here. Second, the personal and caring tenor of Boaz's perspective on Ruth throughout the story weighs against his speaking of her as mere property, regardless of the terminology he chooses. Most important, the selection and repetition of the verb appears to serve a specific rhetorical purpose. As explained above (at 3:9b), the verb "to redeem" does not apply to marriage, so Boaz cannot properly use this verb with regard to Ruth. On the other hand, verbs more commonly used for marriage (*lqh*, cf. 4:13; *nś'*, cf. 1:4) do not fit with the redemption of land. The application of the single verb "acquire" to both transactions

73

underlines the intimate connection between rights and obligations that Boaz is lifting up. He has promised Ruth to resolve the issue of her marriage, and with the help of this rhetorical flourish he resolves the matter of Naomi's (Elimelech's) land as well.

Declaration of the Decision (4:7–10)

The agreement between the next-of-kin and Boaz is formalized by a ritual in which the next-of-kin removes his sandal and gives it to Boaz. The storyteller explains this ritual as a "custom in former times" (v. 7), one with which hearers apparently were not expected to be familiar. This narrative aside plays a significant role in the debate over the date of the book as a whole. As various scholars have shown (see summary in Bush, pp. 27–29), verse 7 contains a higher concentration of expressions typical of post-exilic Hebrew than does the rest of the book. It has been argued that this verse may be an interpolation to help later readers understand what was meant by the action of the next-of-kin in verse 8. This argument for verse 7 as a late interpolation into an old text falters, however, because the clearly late Hebrew phrase for removing the sandal appears not only in verse 7 but also in verse 8. It therefore seems more likely that the storyteller (not an interpolator) is explaining an aspect of a traditional story that was unfamiliar in the time of the storyteller, or that the storyteller is creating an "antiquarian" effect by invoking what was supposed to be a bygone practice. The removal of the sandal does not appear essential to understanding the conversation between the two characters or any subsequent actions in the narrative, so its primary purpose from a literary perspective is to add drama, gravity, and a sense of formal finality to the decision of the next-of-kin.

Removal of the sandal as part of a legal proceeding appears elsewhere only in Deuteronomy 25:9 (where a different verb is used). Although some interpreters have tried to draw formal connections between the two passages because the Deuteronomy passage also contains the theme of preserving the name of a dead husband (25:6) and because Deuteronomy also speaks of what transpires in the presence of the elders at the gate (25:7), the circumstances differ significantly. The Deuteronomy text concerns what a widow should do if her husband's own brother does not take up his obligation to marry her to provide a child on behalf of the dead husband. There the primary legal issue is levirate obligation, whereas in Ruth the primary legal issue is land redemption. There the brother's sandal is removed not by its wearer, but by the widow; in Ruth the sandal is removed by its own wearer. There, although removing the sandal may have ritual significance in confirming the widow's freedom from obligation, the emphasis is that the

74

brother himself has "refused" his obligation to marry her; and the associated gesture of spitting in the brother's face suggests his public humiliation as much as a legal transaction. In Ruth, by contrast, the decision of the next-of-kin is described in terms of his being "unable," not in terms of his refusal to act. The literary structure of the book as a whole confirms this distinction by paralleling the next-of-kin to Orpah: he, like Orpah, chooses an acceptable option in terms of public opinion, while Boaz, like Ruth, goes beyond the call of duty.

Nevertheless, even though the practice of removing the sandal described in Ruth cannot be formally related to that of Deuteronomy 25, the intertextual connections are provocative and may be intentional if we suppose that the storyteller knew of the Deuteronomy text. Both texts do, after all, involve finalizing the decision of a kinsman of some degree not to marry the widow of a dead relative. Although the practice of removing the sandal is explained in 4:7 in relation to the technical language of redemption, which applies to land but not to marriage (see comment on 3:9b, 11–12), the next-of-kin does resume Boaz's terminology of "acquire" when he draws off his sandal, thus tying together the relinquishing of land and marriage. Also, although a distinction should be drawn between "refusing" a duty (Deut. 25:7) and being unable to accept an obligation (NRSV "I cannot," Ruth 4:6), the common vocabulary of being "unwilling" does appear in Deut. 25:7 (NRSV "has no desire") and Ruth 3:13.

The connection between the land redemption and the marriage is continued in verses 9–10 as Boaz declares before the witnesses the essential content of the transaction. Again he ties together the two components by use of the verb "acquire." Here he elaborates his previous statements of the transaction, first by giving the names of Elimelech's two sons, then by identifying Ruth as "the wife of Mahlon" rather than as "the widow of the dead man" (v. 5). Reference to "all that belonged to Chilion and Mahlon" does not expand the amount of land under consideration, but rather reminds the hearers of the course of inheritance that would have been in effect if they had not died. Through Boaz's words we also learn for the first time which of the two sons was Ruth's husband. The meaning of "to maintain the dead man's name on his inheritance" is also given rhetorical expansion (v. 10b). Scholars debate how in actual practice the name of the dead man would "not be cut off," since the biblical genealogies use the name of the actual blood father Boaz rather than the name of the dead husband Mahlon. At least, the remembered and retold story of this widow's marriage to a kinsman meant that the name of her dead husband would be remembered both in his family ("kindred") and in his community ("the gate of his native place"). In this sense a name remembered is a name not cut off.

Finally, it should be noted that Boaz is here consistent in identifying

Ruth as "the Moabite" (v. 10, cf. v. 5). Elsewhere this term appears on the lips of the overseer of the reapers (2:6) and numerous times in the words of the narrator. Why should Boaz include this ethnic designation here? Possibly the fact that Ruth is not an Israelite meant that she was not obligated to enter marriage with a kinsman; but it is far from certain that even an Israelite widow would be obligated under the particular circumstances here (see above), and in any case the question of Ruth's rights or duties does not seem to be pertinent to the events at the town gate.

It seems more likely that the reference to Ruth's ethnic background serves a dramatic and rhetorical purpose. Given Israel's generally negative attitude toward Moabites (see comment at 1:2), Boaz deliberately brings to the fore, rather than ignoring or obscuring, what is likely in the minds of his listeners. If the story was told in post-exilic times to challenge religious opposition to intermarriage (see Introduction), then the point is highlighted here for the ancient listener. For modern readers in almost every culture, the issue of marriage across certain racial, ethnic, or cultural lines remains lively in families and in larger communities. Boaz's approach suggests that such matters should be named aloud, rather than pretending they do not exist. Of course it is possible that his prominence (2:1) in the town emboldened him to take a risk from which others might have shied away. How much he may have swayed private community opinion cannot be known, but the subsequent expression of blessing by those at the gate reflects support for his action.

Witnessing and Blessing (4:11–12)

In response to Boaz's "You are witnesses," those gathered give formal affirmation of their role as witnesses to the agreed arrangements and then offer words of blessing for Boaz's impending marriage. As noted above, those named as witnessing are an expanded group by comparison to those mentioned initially in the episode. Here the elders are grouped together (rather than being divided into ten plus other elders) and "all the people" are added and indeed mentioned first. The importance of the event for the whole community is highlighted, although one cannot be certain whether the expression was intended to include women of the village. On the one hand, the women may not have been regarded as competent formal witnesses; on the other hand, there is no reason to suppose that they might not have gathered round in a public area to hear the men's deliberations, and they certainly were able to offer expressions of blessing, as they do in the concluding scene of the story. The words of the blessing are addressed to Boaz, not to the couple (Ruth and Naomi are not present); but the first phrase especially contains a wish for Ruth herself. The blessing as a whole begins to tie together all the parts of the story, looking back to the introductory words of 1:1 and ahead to the concluding genealogy (4:18–22).

The community expresses its prayer that Ruth, identified not by name but as "the woman [or wife] coming into your house," will fulfill the same role as Rachel and Leah. These two wives of the ancestor Jacob "built up the house of Israel" by bearing between them eight of the twelve sons remembered as progenitors of the twelve tribes of Israel. (The other four were born to the maids of the two ancestral wives, cf. Genesis 29:31–30:24; 35:16–26.) At stake in the building up of Boaz's house is not primarily numbers of children, but rather the importance of the offspring of this union for the future of the people. How remarkable that Ruth the Moabite is compared to Rachel and Leah, for Jacob was sent to their father to seek a wife precisely so that he would be sure *not* to marry a non-Israelite (Gen. 28:1–2)! Like Boaz's explicit reference to Ruth's Moabite ethnicity, this part of the prayer uplifts her in a way that challenges such marriage restrictions.

The reference to the "building up" of the "house" also calls to mind another biblical tradition. In II Samuel 7, God rejects David's plan to build a "house," that is, a temple, for God and promises instead to build a "house," that is, a household of descendants and ruling dynasty, for David (II Sam. 7:27; cf. Ps. 89:4 [Heb. v. 5]). Thus the phrasing of the people's blessing in Ruth foreshadows the eventual rise of David's line and points to the references to him in the concluding verses of the story. Any marriage entered into for the sake of preserving a dead man's name is intended to "build up" his house (Deut. 25:9). In the case of Ruth and Boaz, the consequences of that building up will be extraordinary, paralleling in importance the founding of the people through the sons of Jacob in the ancestral period.

The next section of the prayer refers to the place names Ephrathah and Bethlehem. This terminology clearly connects with the same usage in the opening verses of the story; the use of Ephrathah alongside the usual town name provides a clear allusion to King David (see commentary at 1:2). The NRSV translation "produce children" represents a Hebrew expression involving the term *ḥayil*, which has already appeared in connection with Boaz at 2:1 and Ruth at 3:11. As indicated in the commentary at those points, the word has connotations of wealth, power, strength, valiancy, prominence, and moral worthiness. The NRSV translation here is dependent upon the surrounding references that seem related to procreation, but it unduly narrows the range of meaning carried by the Hebrew. Phrases such as "act worthily," "gain prominence," "achieve prosperity," or "do valiantly" are also implicit here; English lacks a single term that can carry all the possible nuances of the people's words of blessing.

The blessing concludes with references to Perez, Tamar, and Judah. This part of the prayer points specifically to the concluding genealogy (4:18–22), where we learn that Perez is the ancestor of Boaz and David. The descendants of Perez are remembered in two post-exilic texts (I Chr. 9:4; Neh. 11:4, 6) as a specific group of returned exiles living in the city of Jerusalem. Indeed, Nehemiah specifies that these descendants numbered 468 "valiant warriors" (i.e., men of *ḥayil*, the same term that appears in the previous phrase of the blessing in Ruth). The reference to Perez thus points to the line through Boaz to David, but may also have had special pertinence to post-exilic listeners.

The final phrase goes beyond the name Perez, however, to refer explicitly to his mother and father, Tamar and Judah. The striking story of the birth of Perez is recorded in Genesis 38. In brief, Judah (one of Jacob's sons by his wife Leah) selects Tamar as wife for the eldest of his three sons. This first son dies before the birth of an heir, so Judah instructs his second son to perform the levirate duty of impregnating Tamar with an heir for the dead elder son. The second son pretends to cooperate but spills his semen on the ground; soon he also dies. Judah is fearful that these deaths are Tamar's fault (although the narrator is explicit that each son has died for his own misdeeds) and sends Tamar away rather than give his third son to her as the law required. Eventually Tamar takes into her own hands the matter of an heir for her husband. She disguises herself as a prostitute, stations herself where Judah will pass by, and takes his signet and cord as a pledge of payment for her services to him. When some months later she is found to be pregnant and Judah sentences her to death for her whoring, she produces Judah's artifacts and he realizes what has happened, saying "she is more in the right than I, since I did not give her to my [third] son Shelah" (Gen. 38:26). Perez is one of the pair of twins born of this unusual union.

Various resonances with the story of Ruth are immediately apparent. The stories have in common the theme of a widow and concern for an heir for a dead husband. In both stories, two brothers die. In both stories, a widow chooses to approach an older man in a socially unacceptable way in order to effect a change in the situation. Most likely it is especially this last point that leads to the inclusion of the reference to Judah and Tamar in Ruth.

Yet the differences between the stories should be noted as well.

The concern for an heir is central to the Genesis story and to Tamar's purpose in making herself available to Judah; but in Ruth the matter of an heir is not introduced by Ruth, but only by Boaz and the people gathered at the town gate, and there does not seem to be a legal obligation of marriage either for her or for a kinsman (see comments above). While the Ruth narrative does not provide an explanation for the death of Mahlon and Chilion, the Genesis story explicitly treats the men's deaths as divine judgment for wrongdoing. Furthermore, the unconventional actions of the two women are not fully parallel. Tamar deliberately seeks a sexual encounter, whereas the Ruth narrative leaves the impression that intercourse at the threshing floor was possible but was deliberately avoided. Judah, although a widower at the time of his sexual encounter with Tamar, never marries Tamar or even has intercourse with her again, whereas Ruth's child is conceived within the context of marriage to Boaz.

The connections between the stories were no doubt intriguing to the rabbis in later Jewish tradition, for some legends about Boaz add elements to make his story more like that of Judah and Tamar. According to those traditions Boaz (like Judah) was a widower, his first wife having died on the day that Naomi and Ruth arrived in Bethlehem, and Boaz himself died immediately after the night of his wedding to Ruth, thus (again like Judah) having no further sexual relations with Ruth after their child was conceived. (See Darr [pp. 61–71] for a convenient summary of rabbinic interpretation.)

Beyond similarities and differences in detail, in both stories the eventual outcome of a woman's challenge to societal norms is a child whose parentage is reckoned to the actual blood father, not to the mother's dead husband; and both stories belong to the genealogical heritage of King David. When the Gospel according to Matthew reviews the genealogy of "Jesus the Messiah, the son of David, the son of Abraham" (1:1), only four mothers are selected for mention in the midst of the long list of male ancestry, even though many more mothers' names were available in the Hebrew scriptures. Two of these are Tamar and Ruth, the other two are Rahab (listed as the mother of Boaz, although this is nowhere attested in the Old Testament itself) and "the wife of Uriah" (Bathsheba, mother of Solomon). As explained in the Introduction, Matthew's genealogy uses this mention of Ruth and the other women to prepare the way for the extraordinary event of Mary's conception of Jesus apart from Joseph (Matt. 1:18, 20); at the same time, by these women the genealogy foreshadows Jesus' mission to the Gentile community and the openness of the early Christian community to non-Jewish worshipers.

Ruth 4:13
The Household of Boaz

In one brief verse, just fifteen words in Hebrew, the narrator reports the marriage of Boaz and Ruth, their conjugal union, her conception, and the birth of a male child. Once the drama of the morning at the town gate is ended, the story rushes almost headlong toward its conclusion. Yet this terse summation includes the highly significant note that "the LORD made her conceive." God is portrayed only twice in Ruth as an actor intervening directly in human affairs. In 1:6, God gives food to the people of Bethlehem; here God gives conception. Each divine intervention reverses a condition over which human control in the ancient world was limited at best; together they frame the main story as it progresses toward the resolution of the dual problems of famine and death of the male line set forth in the opening paragraph. The provision of food sets Naomi's face back toward Bethlehem, and the ensuing chain of human events, with God ever behind the scenes but invoked regularly in thanksgiving or intercession, culminates with the marriage. But the conception of a child could not be taken for granted. The community's words of blessing at the town gate, with its prayer for offspring and a "name in Bethlehem," (vv. 11–12) were surely spoken with the knowledge that Ruth had been married to Mahlon as long as ten years (see comment on 1:4) without bearing a child.

God gives conception, but the marriage union would not have happened apart from a preceding sequence of extraordinary acts on the part of the human characters, most especially Ruth and Boaz. To be sure, these actions do not appear in the end to harm the self-interest of the characters, and we are not given access to possible secret motives. But the narrator's assessment and also the characters' assessments of one another focus on concern for others. Both the loyal, faithful, and upright action of human beings and special moments of caring divine intervention are necessary along the road to a peaceable community.

Ruth 4:14–17
The Women and Naomi

In a reprise and reversal of 1:19–21, the women of Bethlehem are again pictured in conversation with Naomi. This time, however, the women speak while Naomi listens; this time, the words are of joy rather than calamity; this time, Ruth is highlighted rather than ignored. Probably their words are not intended to convince Naomi to change her perception, for that change had already begun when Ruth reported her meeting with Boaz in the gleaning field (contrast Fewell and Gunn [pp. 80–82], who conclude from Naomi's silence in this final scene that she never abandons her ambivalent attitude toward Ruth). Rather, by confirming what Naomi too can see has taken place, the women's words set forth the new state of affairs in which God's way with Naomi is dramatically different from what Naomi had reported upon her arrival in Bethlehem.

Addressing Naomi, the women bless the LORD for providing a "next of kin" or "redeemer" (*gō'ēl*) for her. Although some have argued that this redeemer must be Boaz, several lines of evidence make it far simpler to read the word as a reference to Ruth's child. First, the women's pronouncement follows directly on the birth of the child, not on the marriage. Second, the pronominal referent to the redeemer continues without interruption to the end of v. 15, where he is described as born of Ruth. Third, the women hope that his name will be famous in Israel, thus expanding the horizon of the previous blessing at the gate that looked for a child to "bestow a name in Bethlehem."

What then is meant by describing the child as "next-of-kin" or "redeemer" for Naomi? This is of course the same term that Naomi and Ruth each used to describe Boaz (2:20; 3:9b) and that Boaz used for the nearer kinsman (3:12) who subsequently bowed out in the proceedings at the town gate. Here the word is used as Ruth used it, not in the technical sense of land redemption, but rather with general connotations of care for a weaker member of the family. This sense of the term is developed in the dual expressions "restorer of life" and "nourisher of your old age."

The idiom "restorer of life" is known from a variety of other contexts that suggest the richness of the image. It can be used in the literal sense of physical restoration from the brink of death (Job 33:30) or for the effect of food in the face of starvation (Lam. 1:11, 19). This more literal sense of the phrase is picked up in the companion term "nourisher," which appears to refer specifically to physical sustenance (cf. I Kings 4:7; Gen. 45:11). In figurative use, "restorer of life" is given a variety of translations to express its nuances. It is used of a comforter "to revive my courage" (Lam. 1:16), of God's law that "revives the soul" (Ps. 19:7 [Heb. v. 8]), and of God's work as the Divine Shepherd who "restores my soul" (Ps. 23:3, although here the verb is used in a different conjugation). The women's choice of this phrase is especially significant because the verb here translated to "restore" means more literally to "bring back." It is exactly the verb that Naomi used in her words to the women in 1:21, expressing her despairing perception that the LORD had brought her back empty, bereft of (male) family members and thus bereft of economic livelihood and of the possibility for descendants. Now the LORD is blessed for the reversal of Naomi's situation. Emptiness has become fullness as faithful members of the community have prepared the way and God has provided conception. It is not necessary that the baby grow old enough to work and provide material economic support for Naomi before the women's pronouncement can be fulfilled, although that more literal dimension is certainly present. The effect of the redeemer child as restorer of life (soul) is already underway by his very existence, as Naomi cradles him and his presence restores and revives her soul.

The women go on to assert that Ruth, who "loves" Naomi, is "more to [Naomi] than seven sons." Seven here represents the traditional number of idealized perfection. When Naomi returned, she viewed the death of her husband and sons, especially at a time in life when she was unable to bear more children, as God's harshness and calamity; she ignored Ruth, speaking as if Ruth were not present. Now the women extol the loyalty of Ruth in terms that, like their description of the child, continue to recall and reverse Naomi's previous evaluation of her condition.

Why is Ruth so esteemed? Surely not just because she happens to have borne this male child. Indeed, the Hebrew syntax stands against such a narrow reading, as does the reference to Ruth's love for Naomi. Rather, Ruth is of such great value to Naomi because everything that she has done from the first scene until now has led to the possibility of the birth of this child of hope. It is Ruth's faithfulness, kindness, loyalty to Naomi, in a word, Ruth's *hesed,* that has led to this outcome. The placing of Ruth above the value of seven sons gives the strongest possible cultural expression of her worth in a society that placed such great value upon male offspring.

This special praise of Ruth yields yet another resonance with the story of her famous descendant, King David, for it is in the account of the relationship between David and Jonathan that the two words love and loyalty (*hesed*) again appear together. To be sure, the context is changed from the familial to the political, and the verb "to love" is used there not just to express personal affection but with additional connotations of political alliance. Yet David speaks of Jonathan in words strikingly parallel to the words of Naomi's neighbor women about Ruth. As he mourns Jonathan's death, David says "your love to me was wonderful, passing the love of women" (II Sam. 1:26). Only here in the Old

Testament is the loyal affection of a man described as better than relationships with women, and only in Ruth is the loyal affection of a woman described as better than relationships with men (Sakenfeld, "Loyalty and Love," pp. 220–29).

The description of Naomi's action following the women's speech raises several questions. First, what does it mean that Naomi, who has declared herself beyond the years of childbearing and indeed has not borne a child in decades, becomes the baby's "nurse"? It is clear from the use of similar terminology in related passages that Naomi with the child at her "bosom" is not to be understood as miraculously breast-feeding this infant. While the term can be used in connection with a sucking child (Num. 11:12), it is also used for the female caretaker of a five-year-old, where the idea of a wetnurse seems unlikely (II Sam. 4:4). The existence of a parallel masculine form of the noun (e.g., for Mordecai's relationship to Esther, Est. 2:7) also indicates that an intimate caring relationship can be intended here. Yet the tenderness of the image, as of a mother tenderly cradling her precious newborn, should not be lost. Naomi, against all her own expectations, is pictured at the last in such a pose.

Second, from whom did Naomi "take" the child? Was Ruth also present for this event, even though she is not named? Is this "taking" merely a general expression, referring to picking up the child? Or is something more formal, such as adoption, at stake, by analogy to a man's "taking a woman" as an idiom for marrying her? Although some have argued that the text represents adoption, based more on the subsequent phrase "a son has been born to Naomi," the arguments are strained and the alleged parallels not convincing. Quite apart from formal adoption, however, the transfer of the child to Naomi both physically and in the symbolic statement that he is "born" to her is distressing to many women from cultures (such as those of traditional Taiwan or Japan) in which authority for the rearing of children has been vested in their paternal grandmother, with the mother having little or no opportunity to participate. Even in Western cultures, disputes between mothers and grandmothers over child rearing are commonplace, as stories in women's magazines, letters to newspaper advice columns, and calls to radio psychologists make abundantly clear. It is therefore important to recognize that the text does not tell us anything about the respective roles of Ruth and Naomi in rearing the child, much less reflect any general cultural pattern of child rearing in Israel. Rather, the point of Naomi's holding the child and of the women's proclamation that he is "born" to her is to highlight the reversal of Naomi's opening lament over her childlessness (1:11).

83

Finally, what (if anything) does Naomi's action signify for genealogy and inheritance? In this connection, it should be noted that except for reference to "renown in Israel," all direct and even indirect reference to the theme of "the dead man's name" and his "inheritance," so prominent in the scene at the gate, disappears in the concluding women's scene and indeed was not mentioned by Naomi in lamenting her condition in chapter 1. Although at first glance it might appear that attributing the child's birth to Naomi resumes that theme, in fact it was Mahlon's line that Boaz sought to continue (4:5, 10). Only by indirection does the child continue the line of Elimelech, and in fact his male parentage is always reckoned to Boaz. In the women's perspective, it is emotional and physical security for Naomi that is of paramount concern, not the preservation of a family name.

The naming of the child in verse 17 is unusual in several respects. Uniquely in the Old Testament, he is named by the neighborhood women, not by either of his parents. Statistically it is more frequently the mother who names the child, rather than the father. Sometimes God gives instruction concerning the name of a child, but the community does not have such a role other than in this passage. Furthermore, the words of the women ("a son has been born to Naomi") do not manifest any clear relationship with the name Obed given to the child. Most often words spoken in connection with naming involve a word play of similar sounds, but that is not the case here. Sometimes the connection is one of a concept or idea, but efforts to develop such a thematic connection are not thus far convincing. If the women's words do not explain the child's name, perhaps they are intended to explain the unusual circumstance noted above: why neither Ruth nor Boaz is naming the child. As the women lift up the child's relationship to Naomi, they may take on the power to give a name as well.

The narrator now concludes this section with five brief words of genealogy that confirm hints already given and bring the story forward to David, a central and revered figure in every subsequent era of Judean history. It is this reference to David that gives the story its "punch," but as explained in the Introduction, scholars dispute whether the story is intended as a defense of David's royal dynasty or as a defense of the inclusion of outsiders in the community. There the case for the latter option is argued: if the great David, chosen by God, had a Moabite ancestor so worthy as Ruth, then surely such women should not be excluded in principle from the Judean community. If Boaz's actions on Ruth's behalf are meritorious, then Judeans of later times who seek to include such outsiders should be supported. Because of David's stature in Judean tradition, just the mention of his name is sufficient to drive home the storyteller's point of view.

84

Ruth 4:18–22
A Longer Genealogy

The book of Ruth concludes with a longer genealogy of David that begins with Perez (cf. 4:12). Although straightforward on the surface, the list bristles with technical problems. Scholars are divided over whether the genealogy is original to the story or was appended by a later hand. The reasons given in support of each view are intertwined with theories about the date and purpose of the book explained in the Introduction. Here the comments will focus on the contribution of the genealogy to the meaning of the final form of the story.

The seventh position in a genealogical list is often significant in ancient Near Eastern tradition, being reserved for an ancestor due special honor; here the name of Boaz is in the seventh position. The tenth slot, here given to David, may also be a numerical indication of special honor. The total number of names in the Ruth list could have been different; for example, it could have started with Judah, father of Perez, for a total of eleven names rather than ten, with Boaz and David moved to slots eight and eleven respectively. Thus it seems likely that the genealogy was designed deliberately to place Boaz and David in their numerical positions, and so to draw the readers' attention to the upright behavior of Boaz, the central male figure of the story, as well as to the significance of the story itself as a part of King David's heritage.

The genealogy also demonstrates that the last section of the blessing prayer on behalf of Boaz (4:12) was amply fulfilled. The house of Perez had other branches, as is known from the genealogies in I Chronicles 2, but it is the line through Boaz that establishes a great house (i.e., lineage), the house of David.

Finally, the introductory phrase, "Now these are the descendants," joins this list to the genre of many such lists in Genesis. The formal and official tone of the genealogy, with its standard introduction, lends authority to the story to which it is attached. Ruth's place in David's ancestry is confirmed, underlined, and valorized in a way that goes beyond the mere listing of Obed's descendants in verse 17. Furthermore, the content of this formal list provides a bridge from the early Pentateuchal stories of Israel to the establishment of the monarchy. Thus in the ordering of books in the Christian canon, the genealogy serves as the literary connecting link to the following book of I Samuel, where the story of David's rise to kingship is told. For Christian readers, of course, the link extends still further: with its specific mention of Ruth (see Introduction and comment on 4:12), the Gospel of Matthew extends this concluding genealogy through many more generations to Jesus Christ, true heir to the house of David, who sends his disciples forth to bring to all nations the good news of their inclusion in God's steadfast love.

HERMENEUTICAL AND THEOLOGICAL POSTSCRIPT

Although the Matthean genealogy of Jesus incorporates references to Ruth and to three other women, the all-male genealogy at the conclusion of the book of Ruth appears to complete a trend toward the disappearance of women characters from the story. As noted earlier, neither Ruth nor Naomi speaks in chapter 4; Ruth is not even spoken to. Furthermore, the genealogy leaves the impression that Ruth is not important in her own right, but only because of her relationship to the Davidic line; otherwise the story of her spunk, grit, and determined faithfulness would not have been worth remembering. Although the genealogy is strictly through the line of Boaz and ignores Mahlon and his father Elimelech, it still reinforces the theme that first arose on Boaz's lips at the town gate, the importance of preserving the names of male members of the community through their descendants.

To be sure, the story as a whole begins with women on their own, making decisions and taking steps to determine their own future; but even these early scenes are implicitly and sometimes explicitly circumscribed by the customs and assumptions of a male-dominated social structure. Thus Naomi's despair is not just that of personal loss; it expands to the inability to provide for her daughters-in-law what is expected by the culture, namely, husbands. Ruth's gleaning represents the option available to destitute women, and the search for longer-range security focuses on the acquisition of a husband, in this case a rich husband. A story with promising beginnings, as women seek to make their own way, ends very conventionally (albeit through unconventional behavior along the way) with the women's security achieved by reintegrating themselves completely into the existing traditional economic and family structures. And it is the men who arrange the details of that reintegration.

How can such a story be read as a word that frees, as life giving, as a text having authority, as a word of good news to readers who see so many human inadequacies in the presuppositions, the processes, and the end result of the narrative? First of all, to the extent that such a critical analysis of the story highlights various shortcomings of ancient Israelite society, readers are challenged to look more closely at their own cultural contexts, to pay more careful attention to the painful points of continuity where comparable circumstances still exist. The commentary has suggested such points of continuity, including migration to avoid starvation, modern forms of gleaning even in urban settings, inadequate governmental welfare systems, limitations on women's rights to own property, the need for well-to-do husbands to ensure women's economic survival. Given the great variety of cultures in which such issues arise, recognizing the continuity between the biblical story and our own broken world seems an appropriate first step. Those who have power to work for cultural change are challenged to transform that brokenness.

Identifying lines of continuity should lead also to the recognition that many people still do what they have to in order to survive. Some people are of course able to work for systemic change in the face of societal brokenness, but not everyone can do that. Where options are limited, people take advantage of whatever possibilities are available and pray that God will see them through. Theirs is of necessity a "theology of survival." (See Williams for a powerful exposition of this theme in relation to the slave-woman Hagar.) In short, the story of Ruth need not, indeed should not, be read as an endorsement of every aspect of its ending as the desire of God for all times and places. It is rather a story of women making a way (at least some sort of a way) out of no way, enabled by God behind the scenes and by other faithful people epitomized by Boaz.

Why then speak of chapter 4 and the story's conclusion as "the peaceable community," when it is so easily criticized for its shortcomings? How can one get beyond the "husband, wife, two children, one dog, one cat" version of "happily ever after" (to use an example from pop American culture)? The answer lies in looking beyond the specific social structures to their underlying principles, much as one may interpret biblical legal material theologically by looking beyond the specific case laws. From this perspective, the story of Ruth embodies a variety of themes basic to the biblical version of human community. *First* of all, no one is to be left destitute. The community is responsible for feeding the hungry. *Second,* loneliness and despair must not be ignored. Recognizing that such emotions are part of the broken human condition, the community of faith is called to acts of healing. Marriage and children are not the only way of responding to loneliness; offers of friendship between adults of the same sex and invitations to participate in the larger community circle can also overcome such isolation. *Third,* children are valued, and so are old people; both are to be held tight and cared for. *Fourth,* the marginalized outsider may appropriately be "pushy" towards being included, and those in the center are called to move toward the margins and the marginalized. Ruth the marginalized Moabite insists on coming where she is not wanted; Boaz the most

87

center-identified Israelite of his town reaches out to her. Yet the location of characters in center or margin is more complicated. The story was first addressed not to a dominant group or culture, but to a small Judahite group, itself marginalized, trying to maintain its communal and religious identity. From this perspective, one may imagine the Bethlehemite community, including Boaz, as the marginalized, whom Ruth as a member of the "center," the dominant non-Israelite and non-Yahwistic culture, seeks to join. Boaz's actions encourage his marginalized community in receiving someone who seeks to depart from the center. Ruth and Boaz, each reaching from margin to center and from center to margin, bear witness to God's desire for every age and community, not just to some ancient debate about ethnic prejudice.

The four themes mentioned above are not intended as an exhaustive list, but as thought-provoking illustrations. Above all, it must be reiterated that undergirding and enabling all these dimensions of this peaceable Bethlehemite community is the loyal kindness of God, who occasionally intervenes but mostly works through the loyalty and kindness of worthy women and men. By their actions Ruth and Boaz give us a glimpse not just of how we should live, but also of what the loyal kindness of God might be like. For Christians that glimpse expands to fullness in Jesus of Nazareth, born of Mary, son of David, descendant of Ruth, Messiah, who fed the hungry, succored the grieving, entered into unlikely friendships, and confounded traditional categories of center and margin. The story of Ruth and the story of Jesus Christ invite us to love loyal kindness and to follow the God in whom dividing walls of hostility are still being broken down.

BIBLIOGRAPHY

For Further Study

Brenner, Athalya, ed. *A Feminist Companion to Ruth* (Sheffield: Sheffield Academic Press, 1993).

Bush, Frederic W. *Ruth, Esther*. Word Biblical Commentary (Waco: Word Books, 1996).

Campbell, Edward F. Jr. *Ruth: A New Translation with Introduction, Notes, and Commentary*. The Anchor Bible (Garden City: Doubleday & Company, Inc., 1975).

Chu, Julie Li-Chuan. "Returning Home: The Inspiration of the Role Dedifferentiation in the Book of Ruth for Taiwanese Women," in *Reading the Bible as Women: Perspectives from Africa, Asia, and Latin America (Semeia* 78), ed. P. Bird (Atlanta: Scholars Press, 1997): 47–53.

Fewell, Danna Nolan and David M. Gunn. *Compromising Redemption: Relating Characters in the Book of Ruth*. Literary Currents in Biblical Interpretation (Louisville: Westminster/John Knox Press, 1990).

Larkin, Katrina J. A. *Ruth and Esther*. Old Testament Guides (Sheffield: Sheffield Academic Press, 1996).

Nielsen, Kirsten. *Ruth: A Commentary*. The Old Testament Library (Louisville: Westminster John Knox Press, 1997).

Sakenfeld, Katharine Doob. *Faithfulness in Action: Loyalty in Biblical Perspective*. Overtures to Biblical Theology (Philadelphia: Fortress Press, 1985).

———. " 'Feminist' Theology and Biblical Interpretation," in *Biblical Theology: Problems and Perspectives*, ed. S. J. Kraftchick, C. D. Myers, Jr., and B. Ollenburger (Nashville: Abingdon, 1995): 247–59.

———. "Ruth 4: An Image of Eschatological Hope," in *Liberating Eschatology: Essays in Honor of Letty Russell*, ed. M. A. Farley and S. Jones (Louisville: Westminster John Knox Press, 1999).

———. "The Story of Ruth: Economic Survival," forthcoming in *Realia Dei: Essays in Archaeology and Biblical Interpretation*, ed. P. H. Williams, Jr. and T. Hiebert (Atlanta: Scholars Press, 1999).

Trible, Phyllis. *God and the Rhetoric of Sexuality*. Overtures to Biblical Theology (Philadelphia: Fortress Press, 1978).

Literature Cited

Beattie, D. R. G. *Jewish Exegesis of the Book of Ruth*. JSOTS 2 (Sheffield: JSOT Press, 1977).

Berlin, Adele. *Poetics and Interpretation of Biblical Narrative* (Winona Lake: Eisenbrauns, 1994).

Bush, Frederic W. *Ruth, Esther.* Word Biblical Commentary (Waco: Word Books, 1996).

Campbell, Edward F. Jr. *Ruth: A New Translation with Introduction, Notes, and Commentary.* The Anchor Bible (Garden City: Doubleday & Company, Inc., 1975).

Darr, Katheryn Pfisterer. *Far More Precious Than Jewels: Perspectives on Biblical Women.* Gender and the Biblical Tradition (Louisville: Westminster/John Knox Press, 1991).

Fewell, Danna Nolan and David M. Gunn. *Compromising Redemption: Relating Characters in the Book of Ruth.* Literary Currents in Biblical Interpretation (Louisville: Westminster/John Knox Press, 1990).

Gaventa, Beverly Roberts. *Mary: Glimpses of the Mother of Jesus.* Studies on Personalities of the New Testament (Columbia: University of South Carolina Press, 1995).

Hals, Ronald M. *The Theology of the Book of Ruth* (Philadelphia: Fortress Press, 1969).

Hamlin, E. John. *Surely There Is a Future: A Commentary on the Book of Ruth.* International Theological Commentary (Grand Rapids, Edinburgh: Eerdmans, Handsel Press, 1996).

Johnson, Marshall D. *The Purpose of the Biblical Genealogies, with Special Reference to the Setting of the Genealogies of Jesus,* 2d ed. (Cambridge: Cambridge University Press, 1988).

Joüon, Paul. *Ruth: Commentaire Philologique et Exégétique.* Subsidia Biblica, 9 (Rome: Biblical Institute Press, 1986).

Kruger, Paul A. "The Hem of the Garment in Marriage: The Meaning of the Symbolic Gesture in Ruth 3:9 and Ezek. 16:8," *Journal of Northwest Semitic Languages* 12 (1984): 79–86.

Lee, Sang Hyun. "Korean American Presbyterians: A Need for Ethnic Particularity and the Challenge of Christian Pilgrimage," in *The Diversity of Discipleship: Presbyterians and Twentieth-Century Christian Witness,* ed. M. J. Coalter, J. M. Mulder, and L. B. Weeks (Louisville: Westminster/John Knox Press, 1991): 313–30.

Meyers, Carol. "Returning Home: Ruth 1.8 and the Gendering of the Book of Ruth," in *A Feminist Companion to Ruth,* ed. A. Brenner (Sheffield: Sheffield Academic Press, 1993): 85–114.

Nielsen, Kirsten. *Ruth: A Commentary.* The Old Testament Library (Louisville: Westminster/John Knox Press, 1997).

Russell, Letty M. *Household of Freedom: Authority in Feminist Theology.* The 1986 Annie Kinkead Warfield Lectures (Philadelphia: Westminster Press, 1987).

Sakenfeld, Katharine Doob. "Loyalty and Love: The Language of Human Interconnections in the Hebrew Bible," in *Backgrounds for the Bible*, ed. M. P. O'Connor and D. N. Freedman (Winona Lake: Eisenbrauns, 1987): 215–29.

———. *The Meaning of Ḥesed in the Hebrew Bible: A New Inquiry* (Missoula: Scholars Press, 1978).

Sano, Roy. "The Bible and Pacific Basin Peoples," in *The Theologies of Asian-Americans and Pacific Peoples: A Reader*, comp. R. Sano (Berkeley: Asian Center for Theology and Strategies, Pacific School of Religion, 1976): 296–309.

Sasson, Jack M. *Ruth: A New Translation with a Philological Commentary and a Formalist-Folklorist Interpretation*. The Biblical Seminar (Sheffield: JSOT Press, 1979).

Steinberg, Naomi. *Kinship and Marriage in Genesis: A Household Economics Perspective* (Minneapolis: Fortress Press, 1993).

TANAKH: The Holy Scriptures. The New JPS Translation According to the Traditional Hebrew Text (Philadelphia: The Jewish Publication Society, 1988).

Trible, Phyllis. *God and the Rhetoric of Sexuality*. Overtures to Biblical Theology (Philadelphia: Fortress Press, 1978).

van Dijk-Hemmes, Fokkelien. "Ruth: A Product of Women's Culture?" in *A Feminist Companion to Ruth*, ed. A. Brenner (Sheffield: Sheffield Academic Press, 1993): 134–39.

Williams, Delores S. *Sisters in the Wilderness: The Challenge of Womanist God-Talk* (Maryknoll: Orbis, 1993).